INTERNAL SUCCESSION:

RETIREMENT SOLUTIONS FOR SMALL BUSINESS OWNERS

by Victoria English

INTERNAL SUCCESSION:
RETIREMENT SOLUTIONS FOR SMALL BUSINESS OWNERS
FIRST EDITION SEPTEMBER 2025
SMALL BIZ COMPANION, INC.

Softback ISBN: 979-8-9995277-0-7
Electronic ISBN: 979-8-9995277-1-4

Copyright © 2025 Victoria English

Cover by **Victoria English**
Edited by **Daniel Ringquist**
with additional editing by **Cody Goodfellow**

To request permission, contact the publisher at: **smallbizcompanion@gmail.com**

Ordering information: **smallbizcompanion@gmail.com**

DISCLAIMER: This book is intended for informational and illustrative purposes only. The case studies, characters, companies, and events described herein are **composite examples,** drawn from a variety of real-life scenarios, personal experiences, and common succession planning patterns. They are **not representations of any specific individuals or businesses,** and any resemblance to actual persons or organizations is purely coincidental.

The author is a small business owner and not a licensed attorney, certified financial planner, CPA, or business broker. **Nothing in this book should be construed as legal, financial, or tax advice.** Readers should consult with qualified professionals before making any decisions regarding business succession, valuation, taxation, or legal structuring.

While every effort has been made to ensure accuracy, the author and publisher disclaim any liability for errors, omissions, or outcomes resulting from the use of this information.

INTERNAL SUCCESSION:

RETIREMENT SOLUTIONS FOR SMALL BUSINESS OWNERS

by Victoria English

CONTENTS

0. Introduction   i-iii

1. The retirement crisis no one talks about   1-18

2. What is internal succession?   19-34

3. How succession works   35-62

4. Making the deal   63-93

5. Financing the deal   93-116

6. Structuring the deal   117-142

7. Legal frameworks that protect you   143-152

8. Transition phases that work   153-178

9. Real case studies (successes & failures)   179-191

10. What happens after the sale   192-214

11. Special scenarios   215-234

12. Final thoughts and next steps   235-247

INTRODUCTION

Tucked into a strip mall, just off Ventura Blvd in the San Fernando Valley, was an unlikely place to find the best chili in Los Angeles. Located next to a U.S. Post Office, patrons would duck in and out of chef Randy Hoffman's little spot to get their fix of his thirty-five flavors of chili. About fifteen flavors were on offer each day, rated one (for not spicy at all) to ten (tongue searingly hot).

Diners came from near and far to patronize Chili My Soul, have a chat with Randy, and sample the day's specials before settling on the flavor that would satisfy their craving. Randy offered all varieties of chili including meat, turkey and vegetarian. He even made an appearance the Food Network's "Chef versus City."

Thanks to his devoted fans, what started out as a strictly take out chili restaurant in the 1980s, had expanded to offer on-site dining. Randy was a fixture, his chili woven into the local flavor pallet. If you were to build a flavor profile for Encino in the early 2000s, Chili My Soul had quickly become a key ingredient, if not an institution.

But when Randy passed away in 2010, the restaurant closed shortly afterward. There was no succession plan in place. What had once been a local institution disappeared almost overnight.

This story is not unique.

Across America, thousands of beloved small businesses quietly vanish each year—not because they weren't successful, but because their founders had no clear path for passing the torch. Many business owners dream of selling their companies when they retire, yet few are ever approached by an angel buyer with a blank check. And often, family members either aren't interested or aren't the right fit to take over.

So what's the alternative?

This book presents a path that too few small business owners consider in time: **internal succession.** That means selling or transitioning your business to someone who already understands it—someone who's helped you build it. A long-time employee. A trusted manager. A loyal team. These people may already be in your corner—they just need a plan, guidance, and the opportunity.

This book explores how internal succession can secure not only your legacy but also the future of your business. By strategically identifying and nurturing leaders from within, you create a pathway for a smooth transition that honors your vision while positioning the company for continued success. Internal succession allows for a more controlled, gradual handover of responsibilities, ensuring that the culture, relationships, and core principles of the business are maintained throughout the transition.

The purpose of this book is to serve as a comprehensive guide for small business owners looking to plan their retirement through internal succession. In the chapters that follow, we will walk you through the process of identifying and developing the next generation of leaders—whether they are family members, long-time employees, or members of your management team. We will delve into various strategies, highlight potential pitfalls, and share practical insights gleaned from real-world case studies. These case studies, woven throughout the book, offer both inspiring success stories and cautionary tales that illustrate the challenges and rewards of internal succession planning.

Whether you are just beginning to consider retirement or are already deep in planning your transition, this book is designed to be your roadmap. It will provide you with the tools and strategies needed to ensure that your business not only survives your departure but continues to thrive, safeguarding the legacy you've worked so hard to build.

1

THE RETIREMENT CRISIS NO ONE TALKS ABOUT

Every year in the United States, hundreds of thousands of small business owners reach retirement age. Many of them have spent decades building something from nothing—sacrificing time, money, and personal comfort to keep their businesses alive. And yet, when it's time to step away, the vast majority of those businesses don't sell.

They simply shut down.

According to data from the Exit Planning Institute, fewer than **30% of businesses listed for sale actually sell.** For small, local, or niche businesses, the odds are even worse. The truth is, most small business owners don't have a plan for what comes next. They assume one of three things will happen:

1. A wealthy buyer will appear and offer to purchase the business.
2. Their kids will take over.
3. They'll "figure it out" when the time comes.

These assumptions are often wrong—and costly.

SECTION 1: THE SILENT FADE OF SMALL BUSINESSES

Every small town has one. The quirky bakery with the lemon bars your mom used to buy. The bicycle repair shop where the same man in grease-stained overalls fixed flat tires for forty years. The family-run nursery where you picked out your first tomato plant. And then, one day, they're gone.

There's no big going-out-of-business sale. No dramatic final chapter. The doors just… don't open again.

In the United States, over **10,000 Baby Boomers retire every day.** Many of them are small business owners. According to the Exit Planning Institute, **75% of business owners regret selling their company within one year,** largely because they felt unprepared or were forced to accept poor terms. But even more alarming: **only 20–30% of businesses that go to market actually sell.** The rest either shut down or are liquidated for pennies on the dollar.

Most small businesses don't have a formal succession plan. Owners are often too busy running the day-to-day operations to think about what happens when they're no longer in charge. Even those who *do* think about it often delay action because of discomfort, fear, or uncertainty.

Here's the hard truth: when a business has no plan for leadership transition, it rarely survives. Without a buyer or successor lined up, a thriving business can vanish almost overnight. Loyal employees lose their jobs. Customers lose a trusted service. Communities lose a fixture of daily life.

And perhaps most tragically, the founder loses the opportunity to harvest the value of what they've spent a lifetime building.

Why Don't Owners Prepare?

Several common reasons keep small business owners from preparing for succession:

1. **They believe they'll work forever.**
   Many owners think they'll just "know" when it's time to leave—or worse, that they'll never really retire. Illness, family obligations, or market downturns often force their hand before they're ready.

2. **They're emotionally attached.**
   A small business isn't just a job—it's a source of identity. Walking away from it can feel like letting go of a child.

3. **They assume a sale will be easy.**
   Most owners think their business is special—and that others will see it that way too. They expect a sale to happen quickly, smoothly, and at a high valuation. It rarely works that way.

4. **They think succession planning is for big companies.**
   "That's for the Fortune 500, not my little family shop," they'll say. In reality, smaller businesses need succession planning the *most*—because they have the least margin for error.

The Impact on Communities

When small businesses close due to lack of succession, the effects ripple outward. Employees who've dedicated years to a business find themselves unemployed. Customers lose a source of trust and familiarity. Local economies take a hit. And in family-owned businesses, relationships can suffer if expectations around succession aren't clearly communicated.

In many ways, this isn't just a financial failure. It's a *failure of legacy.*

But it doesn't have to be this way.

A Common Story: The Closure of Kingston's Copy Shop

For over 35 years, **Kingston's Copy & Print** served a tight-knit community in Upstate New York. Bob Kingston opened the shop in the 1980s and quickly became a go-to for college students, local businesses, and nonprofits that needed quick, reliable printing.

Bob didn't just run a copy shop—he ran a community hub. He helped local teenagers with school projects, printed playbills for the high school theater, and knew most of his clients by name. His longtime employee, Jenny, had worked with him since she was 22.

But when Bob turned 68, his health began to decline. He quietly began looking for a buyer but found little interest—larger print companies didn't want a small shop, and banks wouldn't lend to individual buyers. He never discussed a transition plan with Jenny, despite her deep understanding of the business and obvious loyalty.

When Bob suffered a stroke, the shop closed for what was supposed to be a temporary medical leave.

It never reopened.

Jenny didn't have the capital or legal framework to take over. The equipment was eventually sold off. The shop's lease ended. The community lost more than a business—they lost a piece of their history. All because no one had prepared for the day Bob would leave.

Note on Case Studies:

The real-world examples in this book are fictionalized composites drawn from years of research into small business ownership, succession planning, and retirement outcomes. While the names, locations, and details have been changed, each story is rooted in real patterns and experiences that reflect the challenges—and opportunities—faced by business owners across the country.

SECTION 2: THE MYTH OF THE ANGEL BUYER

Every small business owner, at one point or another, fantasizes about the perfect exit: a stranger walks in, falls in love with the business, and makes an offer on the spot—no haggling, no due diligence, just a handshake and a big check. This fantasy is reinforced by TV shows, startup culture, and the occasional lucky friend who happened to sell their yoga studio to a couple "from out of town."

But for most small business owners, the so-called *angel buyer* is just that—a myth.

The Reality of the Business Sale Market

In truth, most small businesses never sell. BizBuySell's annual Insight Report consistently shows that **only 20–30% of small businesses listed for sale ever actually sell.** The rest are quietly removed from the market, often because there was little interest, unrealistic pricing, or the business simply wasn't ready to be transferred.

Why do so many sales fail before they start? Because buyers—and brokers—look at small businesses through a critical lens. They want businesses with clean books, transferable systems, strong cash flow, and a team that can operate without the owner. Most small businesses don't check all those boxes.

And that's where the dream of the angel buyer falls apart.

Brokers Are Not Magicians

Many business owners believe that once they're ready to sell, a broker will swoop in, list the business, and attract dozens of offers. But professional brokers are highly selective—because their time is their currency.

As seasoned business broker **Len Krick** puts it:

"Listings are not a business broker's 'inventory.' Your time is your 'inventory.' When you 'invest' or 'spend' your precious time on low probability listings, then you get what you deserve and deserve what you get—a low probability of getting a commission."

— **Len Krick,** as quoted in Wit & Wisdom of Business Brokerage, Business Brokerage Press

In other words, if your business doesn't look like a high-probability sale, a reputable broker won't waste their time taking it on. They're not in the business of giving false hope—they're in the business of closing deals.

Before agreeing to represent you, a broker will often do a quiet triage:
- Is your revenue consistent?
- Are your financials professionally managed?
- Can the business function without you?
- Are your systems documented?
- Are your expectations for sale price realistic?

If the answer to any of these questions is "no," your broker may politely pass—or worse, agree to list the business while knowing privately that it probably won't sell.

A Common Case: The Deal That Didn't Happen

Consider the story of *The Clay Nest*, a charming ceramics studio run by Marcy, a talented artist in Colorado. She had a loyal following of students, sold hand-crafted pieces, and hosted weekend classes that regularly sold out. After 14 years, she decided it was time to sell. She called a broker, assuming it would be easy.

But the broker quickly realized the business had no employees, no written procedures, no recurring revenue, and no operational structure without Marcy. Her student base was loyal to *her*, not the studio. Financial records were kept informally, and rent on the space had just increased.

The broker declined the listing.

Marcy was shocked. She thought the business had value—but in the eyes of the market, it was simply a hobby that paid her well. She eventually closed her doors and sold off her equipment.

This isn't a rare story. It's a wake-up call.

What Buyers and Brokers Really Want

Buyers are cautious. They want:
- Turnkey systems
- Documented operations
- A business with value *beyond the owner*

- A team that will stay after the sale
- Clean, verifiable financials
- A clear reason to believe the revenue will continue

This is especially true for buyers using financing. Lenders won't fund a sale if the business appears too risky—and a business that disappears without its owner is inherently risky.

Brokers know this. That's why they carefully vet every listing before deciding whether it's worth their time and reputation.

The Takeaway

The idea of the "angel buyer" arriving with a blank check is a myth. And if your business isn't ready to run without you, then it isn't ready to sell. The sooner you realize that, the more time you have to do something about it.

That doesn't mean giving up on a sale. It means preparing strategically—turning your business into a self-sustaining, documented operation that appeals to the buyers and brokers who *do* exist. Or, as you'll see in the chapters ahead, it might mean turning inward—to the employees and team members who already understand your business best.

SECTION 3: FAMILY ISN'T ALWAYS THE PLAN

For many small business owners, passing the company to a child or relative is the dream. After all, what could be more meaningful than seeing the next generation carry on the business you've built with your own hands? For some, that dream becomes reality. But for many, it doesn't—at least not the way they imagined.

Family succession can be a **powerful and successful path,** but it must be **formalized, structured, and approached like any other business deal.** Without clear expectations, agreements, and accountability, the emotional ties that bind a family can quickly become the very thing that unravels the transition.

The Danger of Assumptions

Many family successions fail because expectations were never made explicit. Owners assume their children want to take over. Children assume they have no choice. Roles remain fuzzy. Emotions go unspoken. The plan feels like legacy—but plays out like improvisation.

Let's look at three examples of how those assumptions can go wrong—and then discuss what *does* work.

Case #1: The Resentful Son

Alan ran a successful masonry business in Pennsylvania. He'd built a strong team and had steady work for decades. His son Eric helped out in the summers and joined full-time after college. Alan assumed Eric would take over eventually—but never said so directly, nor did he offer Eric a formal role in management.

Over time, Alan resisted giving up control, second-guessed Eric's decisions, and dismissed his ideas. Eric became discouraged. Feeling stuck in his father's shadow, he eventually left to manage a commercial construction project elsewhere.

The company limped along without him and closed two years later.

What went wrong? Alan never treated Eric like a business successor—he treated him like a son doing him a favor. Without a written transition plan, equity agreement, or defined authority, resentment built up on both sides.

Case #2: The Daughter with Different Dreams

Maria ran a successful physical therapy clinic in Southern California. Her daughter Sophie worked at the front desk as a teen, studied biology in college, and seemed like a natural heir.

But when Maria suggested that Sophie begin preparing to take over the practice, Sophie hesitated. She had applied to grad school in environmental science and didn't want to run the clinic. She loved her mom's business—but didn't want to be tied to it for life.

Maria had assumed that Sophie's involvement meant interest. The conversation was painful. In the end, Maria sold the practice to a long-time employee. It worked out, but she regretted not having the conversation sooner.

What went wrong? Maria built her dream around her daughter without confirming Sophie shared it. Intentions must be stated out loud. Dreams should be co-authored, not assigned.

Case #3: The Family Fallout

Two brothers, Rick and Sam, ran a successful law firm. The plan was to pass it to Rick's son, Josh. Josh had just passed the bar and joined the firm—but lacked experience and emotional intelligence.

When Josh began making changes to the firm's branding and systems, longtime staff resisted. Sam felt Josh was stepping on toes. Rick defended his son. Eventually, Sam left and opened a competing firm.

The firm split. Clients left. So did the staff.

What went wrong? Josh wasn't ready. Rick failed to prepare him *and* failed to involve Sam in a formal discussion about leadership structure, ownership, and transition timelines. Loyalty to family came before loyalty to the firm—and everyone lost.

Family Succession Can Work

These examples are cautionary—but they don't mean family succession is doomed. In fact, internal succession to a family member can be incredibly successful **if handled professionally.**

The key difference? **Structure.**

Here's what successful family successions have in common:

- A formal plan with timelines and benchmarks
- A written ownership agreement (not just a verbal promise)
- Clear job descriptions and division of labor
- External advisors (CPA, attorney, business broker) involved
- Performance expectations—not assumptions—about the successor
- A plan for mentorship and gradual transfer of leadership

This isn't about removing emotion from the process—it's about adding **clarity and accountability.** When expectations are documented, relationships are preserved. When conversations are honest, resentment has less room to grow.

Ask the Hard Questions

Before planning a family succession, ask:

- Does my child/relative actually want this?
- Do they have the skills or desire to gain them?
- Can I step back without undermining them?
- Are we both willing to put everything in writing?

If the answer is yes—great. Move forward with structure and support.

If not, don't force it. There are other options. The rest of this book will walk you through how to sell or transition to a trusted employee or management team.

Sometimes the most loving thing you can do is **not** hand the business to your child—but to leave them the freedom to choose their own path, and to leave your business in the hands of someone fully committed to its future.

Case #4: When Family Succession Works

Not all family transitions go wrong. Some flourish—when the process is structured like a real business deal.

Lisa owned a second-generation garden supply store in Oregon. Her daughter, Maya, showed interest from a young age and worked in every part of the store—register, inventory, purchasing, marketing. Lisa didn't just assume Maya would take over—she asked, and Maya said yes. But they both agreed: it needed to be formal.

They brought in an attorney to draft a multi-year transition plan. Maya bought in gradually—starting with 10% equity, then 25%, then majority ownership. Lisa stayed on as a part-time advisor for two years before stepping back entirely. They had clear performance benchmarks, profit-sharing agreements, and regular check-ins mediated by their CPA.

Today, Maya runs the business with new energy and vision. Lisa still stops by once a week—but as a proud observer, not a shadow boss.

The key difference? It wasn't a handoff. It was a **professional transition,** built on mutual respect, structure, and communication.

SECTION 4: WHAT IS IT REALLY WORTH?

One of the most emotionally charged—and commonly misunderstood—aspects of succession planning is **valuation.** Many small business owners have a number in mind when they think about selling. Often that number is based on what they've invested, what they need to retire, or a gut sense of what feels fair after decades of hard work.

But buyers don't care about feelings. They care about **cash flow, systems, and risk.**

To plan your exit—especially an internal succession—you need to understand what your business is actually worth, based on standard financial metrics.

Two Common Valuation Methods

Most small business sales use one of two frameworks: **Seller's Discretionary Earnings (SDE)** or **EBITDA.**

1. Seller's Discretionary Earnings (SDE)

SDE is the most common method for valuing small, owner-operated businesses (usually under $5 million in annual revenue). It starts with net profit and then adds back all the discretionary expenses that a new owner wouldn't necessarily keep—like the owner's salary, personal car or travel, meals, insurance premiums, and sometimes one-time costs like equipment purchases or legal fees.

SDE paints a picture of how much money the business really "throws off" to the owner each year.

Sample Valuation Using SDE:
#1: Pet Grooming Business
- Net Profit: $90,000
- Add-backs:
  - Owner salary: $30,000
  - Health insurance: $5,000
  - Travel to trade show: $2,000
- **SDE = $127,000**
- Industry multiple: 2.5x
- **Estimated valuation = $317,500**

#2: Home Repair Franchise
- Net Profit: $60,000
- Add-backs:
  - Owner salary: $40,000
  - Lease on personal truck: $6,000
  - Continuing education seminar: $2,000
- **SDE = $108,000**
- Industry multiple: 2.2x
- **Estimated valuation = $237,600**

#3: Juice & Smoothie Café
- Net Profit: $50,000
- Add-backs:

- o   Owner salary: $35,000
- o   Meals and entertainment: $3,000
- o   Annual bonus: $5,000
- **SDE = $93,000**
- Industry multiple: 1.8x
- **Estimated valuation = $167,400**

2. EBITDA: For Larger or Structured Companies

EBITDA stands for **Earnings Before Interest, Taxes, Depreciation, and Amortization.** It is often used for businesses with professional management, multiple locations, or larger revenues (usually $5M+). Unlike SDE, EBITDA typically **does not add back the owner's salary**—especially if the owner is not actively involved in day-to-day operations.

It's a better fit when buyers want to assess operating performance independent of financing or tax decisions, which makes it popular among financial buyers, private equity, and more sophisticated acquirers.

How to Calculate EBITDA

Start with **net income** and add back:
- Interest (from loans)
- Taxes
- Depreciation
- Amortization

EBITDA Example: Commercial Janitorial Company

- Net Income: $150,000
- Add-backs:
  - o   Interest: $12,000
  - o   Taxes: $18,000
  - o   Depreciation: $20,000
  - o   Amortization: $10,000

- **EBITDA = $210,000**
- Industry multiple: 5.5x
- **Estimated valuation = $1,155,000**

EBITDA Example: Medical Billing Service

- Net Income: $300,000
- Add-backs:
  - Interest: $10,000
  - Taxes: $35,000
  - Depreciation: $15,000
  - Amortization: $5,000
- **EBITDA = $365,000**
- Industry multiple: 6x
- **Estimated valuation = $2,190,000**

EBITDA Example: Digital Marketing Firm

- Net Income: $500,000
- Add-backs:
  - Interest: $0 (no debt)
  - Taxes: $65,000
  - Depreciation: $10,000
  - Amortization: $10,000
- **EBITDA = $585,000**
- Industry multiple: 6.5x
- **Estimated valuation = $3,802,500**

Understanding Multiples

Once you've calculated SDE or EBITDA, you multiply it by a number known as the **multiple.** This is the market's way of estimating **how many years of earnings a buyer is willing to "pay for" up front.**

But here's the catch: **multiples vary wildly** depending on industry, risk profile, location, and even the current economy.

So Where Do You Find Multiples?

- **BizBuySell Insight Reports**–publishes average multiples across industries.
- **IBISWorld and PrivCo**–offer subscription data on private company valuations.
- **Business Brokers**–local brokers often know what businesses in your niche are selling for in your region.
- **Peer Comparables**–you can sometimes find real listings for comparable businesses on sites like BizBuySell, BizQuest, or Axial.

Industry-Specific Multiples (Typical Ranges)

Industry	SDE Multiple	EBITDA Multiple
Auto Repair Shops	2.0 – 2.5x	4.0 – 5.0x
Restaurants	1.5 – 2.0x	3.0 – 4.5x
Medical/Dental Practices	2.5 – 3.5x	5.5 – 6.5x
Landscaping Services	2.0 – 2.8x	4.0 – 5.0x
Marketing & Creative Agencies	2.5 – 3.5x	5.0 – 6.5x
Manufacturing (Niche)	3.0 – 4.0x	6.0 – 8.0x

Note: These are illustrative ranges. Your actual multiple depends on factors like customer concentration, recurring revenue, systems, staff, owner dependency, lease terms, and more.

What Affects Your Multiple?

- **Recurring revenue** = higher multiple
- **Strong management team** = higher multiple
- **Clean, well-documented books** = higher multiple
- **Owner dependency** = lower multiple
- **Unstable or seasonal revenue** = lower multiple

The Takeaway

Valuation isn't just about numbers—it's about telling a clear, credible financial story. Whether you're selling to a family member, a long-time employee, or a third party, your valuation will shape expectations, deal structure, and your ability to exit successfully.

The more prepared you are—with clean books, realistic projections, and a grounded understanding of market multiples—the more control you'll have over your future.

In the next section, we'll dive deeper into **internal succession**— how it works, how to structure it, and why it may be the smartest path for small business owners who want to protect both their legacy and their people.

SECTION 5: PREPARATION PAYS OFF—NOW, NOT JUST LATER

Many business owners resist preparing for succession because they don't feel "ready" to leave. They tell themselves they'll clean up the books, organize systems, and document procedures when the time comes. But here's the truth: those housekeeping tasks? They won't just help you exit smoothly. They'll help your business **run better right now.**

- When your financials are clear and consistent, you make better decisions.
- When roles are documented, your team becomes more independent.
- When your operations are streamlined, you waste less time and money.
- And when your business isn't entirely dependent on you, *you* get to breathe.

Preparing for sale or succession forces clarity—and that clarity almost always leads to **higher profitability, lower stress,** and a **stronger business overall**. Even if you don't end up selling for years, or at all, these improvements pay dividends.

In fact, many business owners report a surprising outcome: once they begin preparing their business to be sold, they fall in love with it again. It becomes easier to manage. It generates more profit. And they begin to see possibilities for growth that once felt out of reach.

So don't think of succession planning as something you do at the *end*. Think of it as something you do to make your business healthier, more resilient, and more rewarding—starting now.

Why Internal Succession Deserves a Closer Look

After looking at the harsh realities of external sales, the emotional landmines of family transitions, and the financial truth about business valuation, the question still stands:

How can a small business owner retire with confidence, protect what they've built, and ensure the business continues?

The answer lies in a strategy that many owners overlook— **internal succession.**

That means turning to the people already in your business: the manager who's held the place together for 10 years. The operations lead who knows every system by heart. The rising star who sees a future in your company, if only they had a stake in it.

These people may not have the capital of an outside investor. They may not have your experience—yet. But they have something more important: **context, commitment, and continuity.**

Internal succession gives you options. It allows you to:
- **Control the timeline** of your exit
- **Mentor your successor** gradually, without walking away cold
- **Preserve your business's culture and legacy**
- **Avoid broker fees or drawn-out sale listings**

- And even, in many cases, **build a passive income stream** by structuring the deal over time

In the chapters ahead, we'll explore:
- How to identify a viable internal successor
- How to structure the deal: equity, payments, contracts, and taxes
- How to protect both your retirement—and your business's long-term success

Because the truth is this: small business ownership isn't just a career—it's a legacy. And legacies don't have to end when the founder retires. With the right structure, support, and mindset, your best decision as a business owner might be your last big one—choosing who takes it from here.

2

WHAT IS INTERNAL SUCCESSION?

SECTION 1: FLAVORS OF INTERNAL SUCCESSION

When most business owners think about stepping away from their company, they imagine a big exit—maybe a strategic buyer, a private equity firm, or a competitor comes knocking with a check in hand. That kind of exit makes headlines. It feels glamorous. But for the vast majority of small businesses in America, that kind of buyer never arrives.

Internal succession offers another path. It's quieter, often overlooked, but in many cases, far more realistic—and ultimately, more rewarding.

Internal succession means passing ownership and leadership of your business to someone already *inside* your company or within your circle. That might be a family member, a long-time employee, a management team, or even a group of employees through a structured buyout. What makes it "internal" is the trust, experience, and institutional knowledge already in place. You're not bringing in an outsider; you're elevating someone who already knows the business from the inside out.

This is not a fallback plan. Internal succession can be *the* plan.

Take Ray, who ran a small independent grocery store in Northern California for over 30 years. He didn't want to sell to a national chain or watch his store get turned into another gas station. His store manager, Ana, had been with him for nearly a decade. She knew the inventory systems, the customers, and had fresh ideas for growth. Ray structured a 20-year seller-financed buyout that would provide him with stable monthly payments for the rest of his life—essentially turning his business into a private retirement annuity. Ana took over day-to-day operations and, within five years, had doubled revenue through community marketing, delivery services, and local product partnerships.

Or consider James, who ran a specialty auto body shop in rural Missouri. None of his kids wanted the business, and brokers told him the location was "too small-town" to attract serious buyers. But his lead mechanic had been with him for 18 years. They structured a transition where the mechanic took over operations immediately and began buying shares over time using business profits. Today, the shop is thriving under new leadership, and James still consults occasionally when a rare vintage car rolls in.

Then there's Mia, who built a thriving dance studio in a major city. Instead of selling to an outside investor, she created a pathway for her three senior instructors to become co-owners. Each contributed a modest buy-in and signed a multi-year agreement to purchase additional shares through profit distributions. This shared structure kept the studio's tight-knit culture intact and created real financial opportunity for her staff. It wasn't just a business deal—it was a legacy.

In each case, the owners didn't chase an exit—they crafted one that reflected their values, relationships, and long-term goals.

There are many flavors of internal succession. Some owners groom a single successor over time, like a second-in-command or adult child. Others create a pathway for multiple employees to buy into the business over several years. Still others explore options like **ESOPs (Employee Stock Ownership Plans) or management buyouts.** We'll cover all of these in more detail in upcoming chapters.

The key idea is this: *You don't need a stranger to validate the worth of your business.* You don't need a press release or a bidding war. What you need is a solid plan, a willing successor (or successors), and a structure that works—for you, for them, and for the future of the company.

In this chapter, we'll dig into why internal succession deserves a front seat in your planning process. We'll explore who your successor might be, why this model works so well, and some of the most common myths that hold owners back from pursuing it. Whether you're looking to retire in five years or fifteen, the decisions you make now will shape the next chapter of your business—and your life.

SECTION 2: WHO COULD YOUR SUCCESSOR BE?

When you picture someone taking over your business, what do you see? A carbon copy of yourself? A family member? A younger version of you with more energy and fewer gray hairs? Or maybe no one comes to mind at all.

The first step in internal succession planning is to open your mind to who that successor *could* be. Because chances are, they're already closer than you think.

Family Members

For many small business owners, the default assumption is to pass the business to a child, sibling, or other relative. Family succession can work beautifully—but it isn't automatic. Not every child wants the business. Not every family member is cut out to lead. And those who are interested may need years of grooming, experience, and outside mentorship to step up with confidence.

Still, when it works, it creates powerful continuity.

Take the story of George Ramirez, who ran **Ramirez Bakery** in Santa Fe, New Mexico, for nearly 40 years. His daughter Sofia had grown up working behind the counter, but after college, she moved to Los Angeles to pursue a marketing career. Years later, during the pandemic, she returned to Santa Fe to help out temporarily—and rediscovered her love for the bakery and the community around it. George wasn't ready to walk away entirely, but Sofia proposed a plan: she would take over operations and begin buying shares from him annually over a 10-year period. Her marketing background helped modernize the business with social media and online ordering, and she introduced seasonal holiday boxes that tripled holiday revenue. Today, **Ramirez Bakery** is thriving, and George receives a stable annual payout while still stopping by for morning coffee and a chat with longtime customers.

Longtime Employees or Managers

Some of the best succession candidates are right under your nose. They've been with you for years. They know your customers, your systems, and your standards. They've probably already been running big chunks of the business while you've been too busy putting out fires.

Look for employees who:
- Take ownership without being asked
- Show strong decision-making skills
- Care about the *whole* business, not just their job
- Want to grow—and have shown loyalty over time

These people may not have capital upfront, but that's where creative deal structures come in. A long-term buyout, profit-sharing, or sweat equity arrangement can turn a trusted employee into a committed owner.

One example is **Deena Walker**, who managed **Rusty Creek Feed & Supply**, a locally owned farm and ranch store in Pine Bluff, Arkansas. When the founder, a retired rodeo cowboy named Rick Nolan, wanted to step back, Deena proposed a structured buyout using a combination of profit-based payments and modest seller financing. She didn't have money in the bank, but she had earned trust—and she had ideas. Since taking over, Deena has added mobile delivery service and monthly clinics on animal nutrition, turning Rusty Creek into a regional hub rather than just a supply store.

Management Teams

Not every business has a single obvious successor. In many cases, a team-based handoff makes more sense. This is especially true in companies that are too large or complex for one person to manage alone—or where multiple individuals bring essential expertise.

A **management team buyout** involves selling the company to two **or more internal leaders, each** of whom takes on a slice of ownership and responsibility. While less commonly discussed than solo successions, these deals are quietly happening all over the country—and they can be surprisingly effective.

Take the case of **Brightside Residential**, a 120-unit assisted living company based in Peoria, Illinois. The founder, Karen Hobbs, had built the business over two decades but knew she couldn't sell it to just one person—operations were too demanding. Instead, she sold the company in thirds to three longtime leaders:

- **Marcus**, the head of facilities and logistics, who had a background in construction and maintenance

- **Allison**, the care director, a nurse with deep relationships with staff and residents
- **Devon**, the business manager, who handled payroll, accounting, and vendor relations

Each contributed a small buy-in and signed a 15-year agreement to pay Karen out using business profits. Together, they created a three-part leadership model that balanced their strengths and kept staff turnover low. The transition was nearly invisible to residents and families—a key goal of Karen's—and the buyout now funds her full retirement.

Management team buyouts require legal clarity, aligned values, and ongoing communication—but when they work, they allow a company to retain its depth of knowledge and distribute leadership across a broader base. They're also ideal for businesses that would struggle to replace the founder with just one person.

High-Potential Junior Staff

Don't overlook junior employees who might seem too young or green. With mentorship and time, they may become strong candidates. In fact, some of the most successful internal successions started with someone who was just 20 years old when they first joined the team—and by 30, they were running the company.

One such story comes from **Grays Harbor, Washington**, where a commercial sign company called **Harbor Graphics** was taken over by a former intern. **Tyler Mendoza** started sweeping floors and prepping vinyl in high school. After a few years, the owner, Mel Carter, noticed Tyler had a gift for design and customer service. Mel began training him in quoting, vendor management, and design software. By age 28, Tyler was managing half the business. At 30, he took over entirely through a structured buyout funded by profits and some SBA support. Mel continues to consult, while Tyler has expanded into digital signage and wrapped vehicles.

Other Trusted Insiders

Sometimes, a successor isn't an employee at all—but someone closely tied to the business. These people often come with industry knowledge, trust, and a deep appreciation for the company's value. Let's look at three examples.

Contractor Buyout

In **Brattleboro, Vermont**, a local furniture maker named **Loft & Timber** was sold to their lead installation contractor, **Eli Stanton**. Eli had worked with the company for over a decade, assembling and delivering handcrafted pieces for clients all over New England. He knew the process, the clients, and the quality standards. When the founders decided to retire, they approached Eli—not because he had capital, but because he had commitment. He bought in gradually, invested in upgraded workshop equipment, and now runs the business with the same emphasis on craftsmanship that made it beloved in the first place.

Business Partner in Another Venture

In **Cedar Rapids, Iowa**, two entrepreneurs co-owned a seasonal corn maze and pumpkin patch. But one of them, **Shannon**, also ran a small on-site coffee kiosk called **Harvest Brews**, which became a local favorite. When her partner **Rachel** decided to sell her half of the main business, Shannon bought her out—folding the event operations under her umbrella. Because she already understood the logistics, marketing, and customer flow, the transition was seamless. Shannon now operates the pumpkin patch and coffee shop as a single brand, with cross-promotion that's boosted both sides of the business.

Vendor Buyout

Sometimes, the buyer is someone on the supply side. That was the case in **Toledo, Ohio**, where a small chain of janitorial supply stores called **ProClean Central** was sold to one of its top product reps, **Lisa Garrison**. Lisa had sold cleaning products to the store for years and had developed a strong relationship with the owner, Don. When Don began looking for an exit, Lisa—who had spent a decade watching which products moved and which ones didn't—proposed buying the business. She used a combination of savings and inventory-backed financing to acquire it and turned the chain into a hybrid retail and B2B fulfillment center with online ordering.

Summary

Identifying your successor is less about finding "the perfect person" and more about recognizing who already understands the business and could rise into the role with support. Whether it's family, staff, contractors, vendors, or partners, your next owner may already be standing in your lobby—or delivering a package to your loading dock.

Continuity of Culture and Service

One of the most powerful reasons internal succession succeeds is that the new owner already understands—and often embodies—the business's culture.

They've worked under your leadership. They know what matters to your customers. They've seen the systems evolve and the challenges emerge in real time. That familiarity reduces the learning curve and minimizes the risk of alienating employees or clients.

When the successor is internal, the *feel* of the business remains intact, even if a few small updates are made. But when the buyer is external, that continuity is far more fragile.

Case Study: The Boutique That Lost Its Soul

In **Ashland, Oregon**, a popular shop called **Larkspur Threads** had built a loyal customer base over 15 years. Its owner, Elise Tran, hand-selected artisan-made clothing and knew many of her customers by name. When she sold to a corporate buyer from out of state, the new owners immediately changed vendors to increase margins, replaced local designers with mass-market brands, and began offering online flash sales.

It made financial sense on paper—but it alienated nearly every long-time customer. Within a year, foot traffic had dropped by half. The staff, demoralized by the changes, began quitting. By year two, the business had closed, leaving a bitter aftertaste for both Elise and the community.

Case Study: A Smooth Cultural Hand-Off

Contrast that with **Sullivan's Automotive**, a family-run auto repair shop in **Chicopee, Massachusetts**. The founder, Tom Sullivan, sold the business over five years to his lead technician, **Kenny Diaz**, who had worked alongside him for over a decade. During the transition, Tom gradually handed off customer service and operations, while Kenny slowly introduced new diagnostic technology and started a loyalty program for repeat clients.

The changes were thoughtful and incremental. The shop still felt like Sullivan's—but better. Longtime clients stayed, word-of-mouth increased, and the business grew 25% in the first three years after Tom fully stepped away. Tom still drops by every now and then, proud to see his name on the building and his legacy in action.

Lower Risk of Deal Failure

One of the biggest hidden advantages of internal succession is that it *dramatically reduces the risk* of the deal falling through.

External sales, even with the most promising buyers, are notoriously fragile. Here's why:

What Can Go Wrong with External Sales

Even when a buyer is enthusiastic, dozens of things can derail the process:

- **Inability to Secure Financing:** Traditional buyers often rely on SBA loans or private lenders. If your business doesn't meet underwriting criteria, the deal dies.
- **Overvaluation by Seller:** Many business owners overestimate their company's worth based on emotion or hearsay. A buyer doing due diligence may uncover weak margins, client concentration risk, or dependency on the owner—leading to a much lower offer or a complete walkaway.
- **Unflattering Financials:** Poor bookkeeping, inconsistent revenue, or cash-based operations can raise red flags. Even if you've been profitable for years, the lack of clean documentation can sink the deal.
- **Legal or Compliance Issues:** Are your licenses current? Do you have documented contracts with employees or vendors? Are there any unresolved lawsuits or tax issues? Buyers will want legal clarity.
- **Customer Concentration Risk:** If more than 25% of your revenue comes from one or two clients, buyers may fear instability if those clients leave after the sale.
- **Physical Asset Concerns:** Are your equipment, vehicles, or facilities in good shape? Deferred maintenance can become a point of contention during negotiations.
- **Key Employee Risk:** If your business depends heavily on a single manager or technician who might quit after the sale, that can scare off a buyer—or drastically reduce valuation.

- **Inventory Complications:** Are you tracking inventory in a system buyers can understand? Is any of it obsolete or unsellable? If they can't verify its value, they won't want to pay for it.

All of this gets uncovered during **due diligence,** which is the buyer's process of scrutinizing every aspect of your business before finalizing the deal.

What Does Due Diligence Actually Involve?

Here's a non-exhaustive list of what an external buyer may request to see:

- **3–5 years of financial statements** (P&L, balance sheets, cash flow statements)
- Tax returns
- Payroll records
- Customer lists and contract agreements
- Leases and property documents
- Vendor agreements
- Loan and debt obligations
- Inventory records
- List of assets and depreciation schedules
- Employment contracts and HR policies
- Intellectual property documentation
- Website traffic data, social media metrics, and ad performance
- Litigation history or pending legal issues

Even if your business is healthy, the process is invasive and time-consuming. If you haven't kept immaculate records—and let's be honest, most small business owners haven't—it can derail the deal or give the buyer leverage to push your price down.

The Intangible Value You Can't Transfer

There's another reason many external sales fall apart—or leave both sides disappointed: **not everything about owning a small business shows up on paper.**

As an owner, you've likely built your business around your life, not the other way around. Maybe you drive a company vehicle. Maybe your spouse's cell phone is on the business plan. Maybe you've structured your workdays so you can pick up your child from school, or take off every Friday without asking permission. You might attend trade shows that double as vacations, or write off part of your home office. You probably enjoy a kind of autonomy, rhythm, and identity that's deeply personal.

These perks and benefits—legal and otherwise—are part of the real value of the business *to you*. But they're nearly impossible to quantify for a buyer.

To an external buyer, your business might just look like a job with a lot of risk attached. If they don't see a clear and documented return on investment, they'll hesitate—or they'll demand a price cut to compensate for the uncertainty.

Internal successors, on the other hand, are already living inside the business. They see the hidden value. They understand the lifestyle benefits. They're not asking, "Can I get my money back in three years?" They're asking, "Can I build a life here?"

That difference in mindset makes a huge difference in how the deal gets structured—and whether it actually closes.

Why Internal Deals Are Less Fragile

Internal successors already know what they're getting. They've seen the financials. They've worked with the people. They've used the systems. They likely aren't expecting perfection—they're expecting continuity and opportunity.

That doesn't mean due diligence disappears. It just becomes more flexible, collaborative, and realistic. Often, internal buyers are more focused on how to make the transition work than on squeezing out every possible risk before moving forward.

Also, many internal deals don't require third-party financing. They can be built on:

- Seller-financed installment agreements
- Gradual equity transfers tied to performance
- Profit-sharing models that scale over time

Because of that flexibility—and that trust—the deal is far more likely to *actually happen.*

And from the seller's point of view, that's everything.

SECTION 3: COMMON MYTHS (AND TRUTHS)

Even when business owners like the *idea* of internal succession, many dismiss it quickly—often because of one of the following myths. Some are rooted in fear. Others come from bad advice. All of them are worth examining.

Myth #1: "No One Wants My Business"

This is one of the most common and most damaging beliefs.

The truth is, someone probably *does* want your business—they just don't know it yet. Most internal successors don't raise their hand until they're invited. They assume the business will be sold externally, or they believe they couldn't afford to buy it even if they wanted to.

When you start the conversation early—before you're ready to retire—you give people time to imagine themselves in the role. You also give yourself time to develop the right person if they're not fully ready today.

You don't need someone who's perfect now. You need someone with potential, values that align with yours, and the willingness to grow into leadership.

Myth #2: "They Can't Afford It"

It's true—most employees don't have the capital to write a six- or seven-figure check on Day One.

But that doesn't mean a deal can't be done.

Most internal succession plans are structured creatively:
- Profit-sharing that converts to equity
- Gradual buy-ins tied to performance milestones
- Seller financing with extended payout periods
- SBA loans paired with personal investment
- Hybrid agreements with deferred payments

Remember, what you need isn't a down payment—it's a plan that ensures you get paid fairly over time. A well-structured internal deal can be just as lucrative (and in some cases *more* stable) than an outside sale, especially when it includes consulting income or phased equity transfers.

Myth #3: "No One Can Run This Business Like I Do"

Maybe not. But the goal isn't to find your clone—it's to find someone who can make it their own *without* destroying what you've built. Letting go is hard. Especially when your business is your identity, your passion, or your legacy. But holding onto control because "no one else can do it" can lead to burnout—and missed opportunity.

You built the business. Now you can build the next leader.

And you may be surprised: many successors preserve what matters most while improving systems you never had time to fix. Their way won't be your way—but it might work just as well (or better).

Myth #4: "I Have to Sell It All at Once"

You don't. One of the great advantages of internal succession is that it allows for **gradual ownership transfer.** You can sell:
- 10% now, 20% in two years, 70% later
- A third each to multiple people
- All of it, but with a 10-year payout

This flexibility is nearly impossible in traditional M&A deals, but very common in internal transitions.

Gradual sales also let you:

- Stay involved during the transition
- Coach the new owner(s)
- Maintain income streams while pulling back

You don't have to disappear overnight. You can design your exit—on your terms.

Myth #5: "It's Not a Real Exit Unless It's a Big Sale"

Many owners dream of a big payday, imagining the moment they walk away with a check in hand.

That happens—but rarely.

Most small business exits involve either:

- An earnout (paid only if certain targets are hit)
- A seller note (paid over time)
- A structured payout over years

Internal succession isn't a "lesser" exit. It's just a **different** one.

Instead of selling your business like a used car, you're transitioning it like a family home—handing it off to someone who values what you've created and will care for it long after you're gone.

In the long run, that may bring more personal satisfaction, more stability, and—yes—more money.

SECTION 4: WHAT'S COMING NEXT

By now, you've seen that internal succession isn't just a possibility—it's a compelling and realistic path forward for many business owners.

You've learned what internal succession is, who your successor might be, and why this path works so well. You've also unpacked some of the most common fears and myths that prevent business owners from exploring it seriously.

But knowing *what* internal succession is isn't the same as knowing *how* to make it happen.

That's where we're headed next.

In the upcoming chapter, we'll walk through the first steps of building your internal succession plan—from identifying potential successors to assessing their readiness and starting the conversation. You'll learn how to prepare your business for transition, how to begin mentoring your successor, and how to create a timeline that makes sense for both your life and your business.

Whether you're hoping to step away in two years or ten, starting now gives you options. It gives you power. And it gives you peace of mind.

You don't need all the answers today—but you do need to start asking the right questions.

Let's begin.

3

HOW SUCCESSION WORKS

SECTION 1: WHEN TO START SUCCESSION PLANNING

The best time to start planning your internal succession is *before* you think you're ready.

Too many business owners wait until they're burned out, facing a health issue, or staring down a looming retirement date before they begin thinking about what happens next. At that point, options are limited. Successors may not be ready. Transitions get rushed. And the value of the business can suffer.

Internal succession is not a last-minute task. It's a **multi-year process** that unfolds best when it starts early—while the owner is still engaged, healthy, and able to mentor the next generation.

Why So Early?

Internal succession takes time because it isn't just about transferring paperwork—it's about transferring leadership, decision-making authority, trust, and culture. That can't be rushed.

You might need time to:
- Identify the right person (or team)
- Develop their skills and confidence
- Shift responsibilities slowly over time
- Create financial structures for the transfer
- Communicate the plan to staff, clients, and stakeholders

None of that happens in a month. Or even six months. In many cases, it takes **three to five years** to fully and smoothly transition ownership.

Starting early also protects you from unexpected events. A medical diagnosis, family emergency, or market downturn can derail your plans if you're not already in motion. A succession plan isn't just about retirement—it's about resilience.

What Happens When You Wait Too Long?

Business owners who delay succession planning often face one of these outcomes:

The Business Closes Down

Case: Garden City Bikes – Missoula, Montana

Owned by **Wayne Reilly**, this beloved local bike shop had served the Missoula community for 28 years. Wayne had always assumed he'd "figure out retirement later," but when he was diagnosed with a rare neurological condition, he had to step away abruptly. With no succession plan in place and no one trained to take over, Garden City Bikes closed within six months. The loss rippled through the cycling community and left Wayne with no ongoing income from the business he'd built.

The Sale Is Rushed at a Discount

Case: Lemont Hardware – Lemont, Illinois

Darlene Shaw had owned Lemont Hardware for 35 years. When her husband passed away suddenly, she decided to retire and sell—but she needed to close the deal fast to handle personal finances. With no internal successor, she sold to a regional chain at 40% below market value. Within a year, the new owners replaced the entire staff and rebranded the store, alienating longtime customers and cutting off Darlene's legacy. She walked away with less than she'd expected—and a business she no longer recognized.

Employees or Family Are Blindsided

Case: Coastal Frame Co. – Mobile, Alabama

Doug Palmer never told his daughter or his shop manager that he was considering retirement. After 22 years in business, he sold Coastal Frame Co. to a private buyer without warning. The buyer immediately laid off half the staff and changed the pricing structure. Doug's daughter, who had hoped to one day be part of the business, was devastated—and the shop manager quit in protest. What could have been a meaningful transition became a fracture in both the family and the business.

The Successor Fails

Case: Pine Ridge Kennels – Flagstaff, Arizona

Maria Gutierrez, owner of Pine Ridge Kennels for 19 years, sold her business to a young employee named Leo—who had potential but no preparation. Maria gave him the keys and walked away within two months, thinking she was "letting him figure it out on his own." But Leo had never handled payroll, licensing, or vendor relationships. Within a year, he was overwhelmed, and the business was in debt. Eventually, he sold to a boarding chain just to get out from under the pressure. With more time and mentorship, Leo might have thrived—but without it, he struggled and lost the opportunity.

You Don't Need to Have All the Answers

One reason business owners put off succession planning is that they feel overwhelmed. They don't know who their successor will be, or how the deal will be structured, or when exactly they want to step away.

That's okay.

You don't need a perfect plan to get started. You just need to begin asking better questions—and being honest about the answers.

Who are the key people in your organization?

Think about the people who understand the business beyond just their job description. They may not be leaders *yet*, but they might become key players with the right development.

Here are three hypothetical examples of who a "key person" might be:

- *Marsha, your office manager:* She's been with you for 11 years. She knows every vendor by name, can recite your pricing model in her sleep, and keeps the books clean—but she hates public speaking and doesn't want to "be the face" of the company. *Potential to become the operations lead in a successor team.*
- *Luis, your top technician:* He's quiet, highly skilled, and deeply respected by the staff. He has zero business experience but everyone trusts him. *Could be part of a multi-person succession, if paired with someone who handles finance/admin.*
- *Arielle, your daughter:* She's 25 and works in marketing for a tech startup across the country. She's not involved in your business—but she's smart, driven, and has expressed interest in "maybe taking it over someday." *Not ready now—but if you start the conversation and bring her in gradually, she could become your long-term plan.*

The person doesn't need to be perfect. They just need to have the potential—and the interest. The rest can be developed with time, mentorship, and a clear roadmap.

If you had to step away for six months, who would take charge?

Let's say your aging parent in another state needs in-home care, and you're the only available family member. You have to leave town with 10 days' notice—and you're not sure when you'll be back.

What happens next?

- Would your staff know who's in charge?
- Would bills get paid? Would the bank accounts be accessible?
- Would the business run smoothly—or just tread water?

Now take it further. What parts of your business would continue automatically?

- **Client scheduling** might roll forward with the help of a CRM or calendar system.
- **Payroll** might auto-run through Gusto or ADP.
- **Inventory** might continue being managed by someone on the ground.

But where might things fall apart?

- **Vendor negotiations**—no one else knows your terms or contacts.
- **Hiring or firing**—no one is authorized to make staffing decisions.
- **Customer escalations**—only you can handle the angry client with a big contract.

And who is missing?

You might realize you don't have a true second-in-command. Maybe everyone reports to you. Or maybe the person who *could* take charge doesn't have access to systems or documents—or the legal authority to use them.

Succession planning begins with *identifying those gaps*.

What tasks or decisions are only made by you?

This is where many owners realize how entangled they are in the business. You might be the only one who:

- Signs contracts or negotiates rates
- Manages the books and pays taxes
- Approves major purchases
- Talks to your accountant, insurance broker, or attorney
- Handles customer complaints personally

Why do you do all of this?

In many cases, it's about **control and liability**. If your name is on the lease and the business license, you may feel like no one else should touch the finances. Or you've never trusted anyone to see the full P&L. Or maybe you're the only one who truly *understands* how everything works.

But these habits—while often reasonable—create serious bottlenecks when you try to step away.

Succession means transferring not just authority but *access*. And that takes planning.

What would happen to your clients?

Let's say you own a **dance studio**, and you've been teaching 80% of the classes yourself for the last 15 years. Your name is on the signage. Parents request you specifically. You choreograph the spring recital and emcee every event.

If you walked away, would clients stay?

If not, it's time to start transitioning their loyalty. That could mean:

- Introducing new instructors gradually
- Creating a brand that isn't just built around your name
- Letting others lead events so the community starts seeing multiple faces in charge

Client trust is transferable—but only if you start the process while you're still involved.

What would happen to your staff?

Some businesses have a formal hierarchy. Others are more flat—but still owner-centric.

Ask yourself:
- Do all employees report directly to me?
- Do I approve every schedule, raise, or disciplinary action?
- If I left, would anyone feel empowered to lead?

In many small businesses, the owner unintentionally becomes the single point of accountability. That works—until it doesn't.

If everyone reports to you, consider building **layers of leadership.** Even just designating a **team lead** or **department head** can begin shifting decision-making down, preparing the organization to function without your daily presence.

SECTION 2: ASSESSING THE READINESS OF YOUR BUSINESS

It's one thing to imagine stepping away from your business someday. It's another thing to know your business could keep functioning—and thriving—without you.

Internal succession depends on more than just finding the right person. Your business itself has to be ready to hand off. That means having the systems, structures, documentation, and clarity needed for someone else to step in and lead. The more reliant your business is on *you*, the harder it will be to transfer—no matter how talented the successor.

This section will walk you through the major areas to evaluate and strengthen before you move forward with any transition plan.

Are Your Financials Clear and Up to Date?

A business can't be transferred—internally or otherwise—if no one understands its financial position.

Ask yourself:
- Are your books current, clean, and professionally managed?
- Do you have a profit and loss statement, balance sheet, and cash flow summary for at least the last two years?
- Can someone other than you interpret them?

Even if you're not planning to sell to an outsider, your successor will still need to understand how the business makes money, where it spends, and where the risks lie. If your books are messy or opaque, it's hard to price the business, structure payments, or ensure a fair transition.

Example: In one small marketing firm, the owner ran everything through a personal account for tax flexibility. But when it came time to hand the business off to a long-time employee, they had to spend nearly six months cleaning up the books just to figure out what the business was actually worth. That delay could've been avoided with better structure in advance.

Do You Have Your Documentation in Order?

One of the biggest succession roadblocks isn't people—it's paperwork.

Your successor needs more than institutional knowledge. They need access to the nuts and bolts of how the business runs.

Key items include:
- Operating agreements or partnership docs (if applicable)
- Tax records and payment history
- Vendor and supplier contracts
- Lease or property agreements

- Insurance policies
- Client contracts or service agreements
- Employment agreements, handbooks, and HR policies

Even if you plan to stay involved for a while, you should assume that at some point, someone else will need to make decisions without calling you. Having this information accessible—and well organized—lays the foundation for trust and accountability.

Are Your Systems and Processes Transferable?

Even the most passionate, capable successor will struggle if the business depends on knowledge that lives only in your head.

For the next month, try this exercise: every time you do *any* kind of work in your business, ask yourself, *"Does someone else know this needs to be done? Do they know how to do it?"* If the answer is no, add it to a running list of processes that need to be documented—even if you don't have time to document them right now.

You don't need to systematize everything overnight. But you should start documenting your most important processes—especially the ones you personally handle.

These might include:
- Invoicing and payment collection
- New client onboarding
- Pricing models or quoting systems
- Monthly payroll processes
- Vendor management and ordering
- Seasonal planning or promotions
- Emergency protocols

Ask yourself: If someone had to take over this role next week, could they do it with what's currently written down?

If not, you have work to do.

Tip: You don't have to create a full operations manual. Start small. Choose one process per month to document, and assign one staff member to test it without your help. This forces clarity—and gives you a chance to improve your systems along the way.

Is Your Business Dependent on You?

This is the hardest question to ask—and the most important.

Is your business a machine with gears that run independently? Or are *you* the engine?

Consider:

- Do clients ask for you by name?
- Are you the only one who handles big decisions, conflict resolution, or pricing?
- Could your staff answer major questions without checking with you?

The more your business depends on you personally, the harder it will be to step away. That's not a judgment—it's a reflection of how most small businesses are built. But succession means intentionally shifting some of that dependence away from yourself.

It doesn't mean becoming irrelevant. It means becoming *replaceable*—in a good way.

Transition Tip: Start introducing other staff members as client-facing contacts. Share decision-making authority. Let others run meetings, pitch proposals, or lead projects. Over time, your presence will evolve from necessary to optional—which is exactly what you want when succession day comes.

Checklist: Is Your Business Ready to Be Transferred?

Use this checklist to evaluate the operational readiness of your business. You don't need a perfect score—but the more boxes you can check, the smoother your eventual transition will be.

Financial Readiness

- My books are current and accurate.
- I have up-to-date profit and loss statements.
- I have up-to-date balance sheets.
- I have up-to-date cash flow statements.
- My successor (or potential successor) could interpret the profit and loss statements.
- My successor could interpret the balance sheet.
- My successor could interpret the cash flow data.
- The business is not run through personal accounts.

Documentation

- I have access to recent tax returns.
- I have documentation of past tax payment history.
- Lease agreements are accessible and current.
- Vendor contracts are accessible and current.
- Insurance policies are accessible and current.
- Client contracts or service agreements are documented and current.
- Employee agreements are documented and current.
- I have an employee handbook or documented HR policies.
- Company bylaws or operating agreements are on file.
- Partnership documentation (if applicable) is up to date and on file.

Systems & Processes

- There is a central location (digital or physical) for storing standard operating procedures.
- I've begun documenting recurring tasks I personally perform.
- At least one team member has been trained to perform some of my regular tasks.
- I have a running list of business processes that are currently undocumented.
- I have tested at least one documented process by asking someone else to follow it.

Owner Dependence

- Clients do not rely solely on me for communication.
- Clients do not rely solely on me for service delivery.
- Another person in the business has decision-making authority in my absence.
- My attorney's contact information is known to someone besides me.
- My CPA's contact information is known to someone besides me.
- My landlord or property manager's contact info is known to someone besides me.
- I have identified which tasks or responsibilities only I can currently perform.
- I have started a plan to delegate or transition those responsibilities.

SECTION 3: EVALUATING POTENTIAL SUCCESSORS

Choosing your successor is the most important decision in the entire succession process. It's not just about identifying someone who's capable—it's about identifying someone who can grow into the role, carry the culture, and earn the trust of your team and your clients.

That doesn't mean you need to find a perfect candidate. No one is perfect. But you do need to know what qualities matter most, what shortcomings are workable, and what flaws are deal-breakers.

This section will walk you through real-world examples of potential successors—some who thrived, and others who fell short. The goal is to help you think clearly and realistically about the people already in your orbit.

What to Look For

Here are a few traits that most strong internal successors have in common:

- **Long-term loyalty** to the business and its mission
- **Strong interpersonal trust** with you and with the team
- **Basic business literacy** or the willingness to learn it
- **Emotional maturity**—especially under pressure
- **Growth mindset** and openness to feedback
- **Cultural alignment** with the values that built your business

But even a great candidate will have gaps. The real question is: *Which gaps can be coached or supported—and which ones will tank the transition?*

Case #1: The Reliable but Reserved Operations Manager

Business: Tideland Tree Services
Location: Sarasota, Florida
Years in Operation: 18
Owner: Doug Franklin
Candidate: Reggie, operations manager

Doug had been running his tree service company for nearly two decades. Reggie had been with him for 14 years. He was reliable, respectful, and knew the job site inside and out. Doug trusted him completely in the field.

But Reggie had never shown interest in client relationships or financial matters. He was great with logistics—but shy with customers and resistant to anything involving QuickBooks.

Doug initially planned to hand the business to Reggie in five years. But after trying to involve him in a few client meetings and estimate reviews, it became clear that Reggie *didn't want* to take on leadership. Doug eventually pivoted. Reggie became the general manager under a different successor—Doug's niece, who had a business degree but no field experience. Together, they now co-lead the company. It only worked because Doug didn't force Reggie into a role he didn't want.

Takeaway: Loyalty and operational skill matter—but leadership can't be forced on someone who's not interested in it.

Case #2: The Enthusiastic Daughter with a Sharp Learning Curve

Business: Bluebird Market Café
Location: Grand Junction, Colorado
Years in Operation: 22
Owner: Carla Medina
Candidate: Her daughter, Lila

Lila had worked the register as a teenager and gone off to study graphic design. In her late twenties, after a layoff and some soul-searching, she came back to the family café. She told Carla, "I think I want to run this someday."

Lila didn't know food costs, labor laws, or how to run payroll. But she knew branding, design, and marketing—and within a year, she'd doubled the café's Instagram following and launched a catering line.

Carla started mentoring her on the business side: inventory, vendor relationships, and staffing. Some of it was a struggle. Lila hated spreadsheets. But she cared. She showed up. And Carla made a plan to sell her 10% of the business every year, contingent on hitting clear milestones.

Today, Lila owns 60% and is on track to take full ownership within two years.

Takeaway: Passion and persistence can outweigh inexperience—if you're willing to mentor and structure the transition carefully.

Case #3: The Charismatic Instructor with Boundary Issues

Business: Coastline Martial Arts
Location: Santa Cruz, California
Years in Operation: 11
Owner: Ken Lim
Candidate: Jordan, lead instructor

Jordan was wildly popular with students. Parents asked for him by name. Attendance went up when he taught. Ken thought he might be the perfect successor.

But over time, issues emerged. Jordan would text clients directly, bypassing the office. He accepted cash "tips" for private lessons. He once suggested launching a summer camp "on the side," using Ken's facility.

Ken confronted him and issued a formal warning—but the behavior didn't stop.

Despite his talent, Jordan wasn't trustworthy. He saw himself as the *star*, not as part of a team. Ken ultimately decided not to move forward with succession. Instead, he brought in a business-savvy instructor from another school who understood boundaries and leadership.

Takeaway: Talent doesn't matter if you can't trust the person with your clients, brand, or business structure.

Case #4: The Underrated Bookkeeper Who Became a Boss

Business: Pennridge Pet Supply
Location: Scranton, Pennsylvania
Years in Operation: 15
Owner: Denise Fowler
Candidate: Amanda, bookkeeper

Amanda wasn't flashy. She was soft-spoken, early to every shift, and meticulous with numbers. Denise had assumed Amanda would stay behind the scenes forever.

But when Denise was hospitalized unexpectedly, Amanda stepped up. She handled vendor calls, payroll, and even managed an inventory crisis—all while keeping the front staff motivated. It was a wake-up call.

Denise began involving her in more strategic decisions. They worked with an accountant to structure a five-year buyout, and Amanda now owns 40% of the business, with plans to take full control when Denise retires.

Takeaway: Sometimes your best successor is the quiet one—watch how people behave in a crisis. That's when leaders emerge.

How to Think About Gaps

Every potential successor will have gaps. Your job is to sort them into two categories:

Workable Gaps	Deal-Breakers
Doesn't know the financials—but eager to learn	Can't be trusted with sensitive info or client boundaries
Shy with clients—but respected by staff	Doesn't take accountability or learn from mistakes
Inexperienced in leadership—but loyal and coachable	Thinks they're entitled to ownership without earning it
Weak at operations—but strong vision and management	Refuses to follow policies or undermines authority

If you're unsure where someone falls, start by **gradually increasing their responsibility.** Give them access to metrics. Let them manage a project. Invite them to a leadership meeting. See how they handle pressure, ambiguity, and accountability.

What you're looking for isn't perfection—it's *pattern recognition.*

Red Flags to Watch For

Not every flaw is a deal-breaker. But some behaviors and patterns should raise concern—and prompt a closer look before you move forward with succession.

These red flags don't necessarily mean someone can't become your successor. But they **signal the need for coaching, clearer boundaries, or a slower timeline.** If left unaddressed, they can become fatal to the transition.

Here are some common red flags to watch for:

1. Resists Feedback or Gets Defensive

You suggest a different way to handle something—and they bristle or shut down. Succession requires growth. If they can't take direction now, they'll struggle later when the stakes are higher.

2. Chronic Lateness or Disorganization

They're great with people, but always scrambling. They forget appointments, miss deadlines, or struggle with follow-through. This can be coached—but it's a sign they may not be ready for the next level of responsibility.

3. Overreaches Before They're Ready

They start asserting authority before it's been earned. They try to "run the show" or undermine others. This can indicate entitlement or a lack of respect for structure.

4. Poor Boundaries with Clients or Staff

They text clients late at night, make side deals, or share personal frustrations with the team. These behaviors erode trust and often grow worse with power.

5. Avoids Tough Conversations

They'd rather let problems fester than deal with conflict. If they can't address performance issues or set expectations, they'll struggle to lead.

6. Is Ambiguous About Their Commitment

They say "maybe someday," but don't act like someone preparing to lead. If you're putting more energy into their future than they are, that's a red flag.

7. Doesn't Take Ownership for Mistakes

When something goes wrong, they deflect, blame others, or disappear. Leadership requires accountability—especially when it's uncomfortable.

What to Do If You See a Red Flag:

- Don't ignore it. Red flags are **invitations to investigate**, not reasons to panic.
- Ask direct questions and observe how they respond to feedback.
- Consider setting **short-term leadership trials** before making long-term promises.
- Document what you see so you can track patterns over time.

Red flags aren't disqualifiers—but they are signals. Pay attention to them. They'll either evolve into trust… or into trouble.

SECTION 4: STARTING THE CONVERSATION

Once you've identified someone who *might* be a good successor, the next step is often the hardest: **starting the conversation.**

It can feel awkward, risky, even vulnerable—especially if you're not ready to make a firm offer, or if you're unsure how the other person will respond. But the only way to move forward is to begin.

That said, it doesn't have to be a big dramatic moment. In fact, it's better if it isn't.

Keep It Low-Stakes at First

Think of the initial conversation as opening a door—not handing over the keys. You're not offering ownership yet. You're exploring possibilities.

Start by saying something like:

"I've been thinking more about the future of the business, and I want to start planning what happens when I eventually step back. I don't have a clear timeline, but I'm trying to figure out who might be the right person to lead it long-term. Would you be open to having that conversation—just to see what we both think?"

This approach:

- Shows maturity and foresight
- Signals that the person is respected and valued
- Leaves room for them to say "not right now" without pressure

If the person expresses interest, that's all you need to go deeper. If they seem hesitant, don't push. You've planted the seed. Sometimes, people need time to imagine themselves in the role before they can step into it.

Maintain Confidentiality (Especially Early On)

This part is crucial and often overlooked: **keep the conversation private**—especially in the early stages.

Even if your intentions are good, succession rumors can spread fast and create unnecessary tension. Employees may worry about job security. Clients may worry about the business changing or losing quality. And if the conversation doesn't go anywhere, you've created waves for nothing.

Until there's a formal plan—or at least clear intent—it's best to:

- Have all conversations one-on-one
- Avoid discussing possibilities with other staff
- Ask the potential successor to keep it confidential as well

You can say:

"For now, I'd like to keep this conversation between us. Nothing is set in stone, and I want to explore the idea before we involve others. If and when we move forward, we'll talk about how to communicate it more broadly—together."

This shows professionalism, preserves stability, and protects everyone's reputations and emotions during a time of uncertainty.

Be Honest—But Selective

You don't need to overshare. You can be transparent about your intentions *without* committing to a specific structure or timeline. This helps avoid misunderstandings, resentment, or assumptions.

It's okay to say:
- "I don't know exactly when I want to retire."
- "I'm not sure yet what a deal might look like."
- "I'm talking to a few people before making any decisions."
- "I'd like to work together to figure out what could make sense for both of us."

Succession is a process. The first conversation is just step one.

What You're Looking For in Their Response

The way someone responds to the conversation can tell you as much as their résumé ever could.

You're watching for:
- **Openness** vs. defensiveness
- **Curiosity** vs. entitlement
- **Follow-up** vs. passivity
- **Humility** vs. ego
- **Alignment** vs. resistance to your vision or values

The right person doesn't have to say "Yes!" right away. But they should take the conversation seriously. They should ask questions. Reflect. Want to understand what would be expected of them. That's a very good sign.

Make a Plan for What Happens Next

If the person is open to it, agree on a next step—something small and specific.

Examples:

- "Let's meet again next month and talk through what leadership might look like."
- "Why don't you shadow me on the business side for a week?"
- "I'll start sharing some financials with you so we can look at what a buyout might involve."
- "Would you be interested in taking on one new responsibility this quarter and seeing how it feels?"

A small step forward keeps the momentum going without overwhelming either of you.

Sample Scripts for Common Situations

Starting a succession conversation is never one-size-fits-all. Here are a few sample phrases to help guide you through specific scenarios.

Scenario 1: You're Not Sure Yet Who the Right Person Is

"I'm exploring what the future of the business looks like, and I'm talking to a few people I respect to get a sense of who might want to step into a bigger role down the line. I haven't made any decisions—I just want to start the conversation with the right people."

Scenario 2: They Seem Flattered but Unsure

"There's no pressure to decide anything today. I just wanted to tell you that I see leadership potential in you, and I'd love to keep the door open for future conversations if you're open to exploring it."

Scenario 3: You Have Multiple Possible Candidates

"I'm in a stage where I'm considering several people and paths forward. My goal is to create a plan that's good for the business long-term. If this is something that interests you, I'd love to talk more and see where there's alignment."

Scenario 4: The Person Isn't Ready Now, But Might Be Later

"I know you're not in a place right now where this makes sense—but I want you to know I've thought about you. If you ever decide you want to step into more leadership, I'd be happy to support you."

Quick Checklist: Starting the Conversation

Use this short checklist to prepare before initiating a succession conversation.

Before the Conversation:

- Have I clarified what I'm actually offering (a discussion, not a deal)?
- Am I committed to keeping this private until there's a plan?
- Have I considered how this person might respond emotionally—both positively and negatively?
- Do I have a realistic sense of their strengths and gaps?

During the Conversation:

- Did I emphasize that this is exploratory, not final?
- Did I avoid putting pressure or promising too much?
- Did I ask open-ended questions to gauge their interest and mindset?

After the Conversation:

- Did I agree on a small, clear next step (if any)?
- Did I take notes on their response and attitude for future reference?
- Am I continuing to maintain confidentiality?

SECTION 5: CREATING A TIMELINE

Once you've identified a potential successor and started the conversation, the next step is to figure out **when—and how—the transition should actually happen.**

Internal succession is rarely a one-time handoff. It's a process that unfolds over years, sometimes even decades. The right timeline depends on your goals, your successor's capacity, and the financial structure of your exit.

There are two broad paths most internal successions follow. Each comes with tradeoffs. The first is a **shorter, faster exit timeline.** The second is a **longer, annuity-style transition** that allows you to turn your business into a long-term income stream.

Path One: The Short-Term Exit (3–5 Years)

This option is best suited to owners who want a relatively quick transition and have a successor who is either well-prepared or highly motivated to ramp up fast.

Overview:

- 3 to 5 years from start to full exit
- Owner gradually hands over operations and exits completely within a few years
- Successor assumes full ownership and begins making buyout payments shortly after operational control shifts

Pros:

- **Faster payout:** You begin receiving money sooner, which can be helpful if you're eager to retire, relocate, or invest elsewhere.
- **Clearer timeline:** There's a defined window for stepping away.
- **Lower emotional drag:** You transition out before fatigue or burnout sets in.

Cons:

- **Heavier financial pressure on the successor:** They'll need to make larger payments in a shorter timeframe, which can strain cash flow—especially if profits are modest or inconsistent.
- **Limited mentorship window:** You may not have time to fully prepare your successor for every aspect of the job.
- **Higher risk of failure if rushed:** If the business or successor isn't truly ready, compressing the timeline increases the chance of missteps.

Best For:

- Owners who have already delegated heavily
- Successors who are ready to lead now
- Businesses with consistent cash flow and simple operations
- Owners who need access to retirement capital soon

Path Two: The Long-Term Succession (5–20 Years)

This approach views the business as a long-term retirement asset. You transition leadership gradually, stay involved strategically, and receive buyout payments over an extended period—functioning almost like an annuity.

Overview:

- 5 to 20 years, depending on business size, revenue, and payment structure
- Operational control transfers early, but ownership and payments transfer slowly
- Payments are often tied to business performance, structured as quarterly or annual installments

Pros:

- **Easier on the business:** Smaller, more manageable payments reduce stress on cash flow and improve the odds of long-term success.

- **Potential for higher total value:** Because you're carrying the risk (not a bank), the successor can afford to pay more overall. Internal buyers often pay a **higher price** than external ones when terms are generous.
- **Income replacement:** You can turn the business into a stable stream of retirement income over 10–20 years.
- **Longer mentorship window:** You have time to develop your successor fully, reducing leadership risk.

Cons:

- **Delayed payout:** You won't receive a large lump sum early on.
- **Requires long-term business health:** If the business falters, your payments may be at risk—especially if they're performance-based.
- **Greater need for trust and structure:** This model requires legal and financial safeguards to protect both parties over time.

Best For:

- Owners who want ongoing retirement income
- Successors who need time to grow into the role
- Businesses with complex systems or long client relationships
- Owners who value continuity and legacy over a fast exit

Choose the Path That Fits Your Goals

There's no universally "right" choice—only the one that fits your lifestyle, priorities, and the nature of your business. Here are a few guiding questions to help you evaluate:

Question	Short-Term Exit	Long-Term Succession
Do I need capital quickly?	√	X
Do I want a clean break?	√	X
Is my successor ready now?	√	X
Is legacy and stability my top concern?	X	√

Question	Short-Term Exit	Long-Term Succession
Do I want income for the next 10–20 years?	X	√
Can the business afford large payments quickly?	√ (if profitable)	X
Can I stay engaged for several more years?	X	√

Hybrid Options Also Exist

Many owners start with a short-term mindset—then realize they'd prefer a slower pace. Others begin planning a 10-year succession and speed it up when things go well.

You can combine elements of both:

- Immediate partial sale + long-term income stream
- Minority equity now, with majority stake transferred later
- Performance-based bonus tied to growth during the transition

Flexibility is key. The best plans evolve with time.

Start Now—Adjust Later

Whether your plan is 3 years or 20, the most important step is to **start.** Your first move might be:

- Delegating one major responsibility
- Bringing your successor into financial discussions
- Outlining your income needs in retirement
- Meeting with an advisor to model cash flow or taxes

Succession is not a single date on the calendar. It's a living strategy—one that grows stronger the earlier you begin.

Your Path Is Taking Shape

Internal succession isn't something you figure out in a weekend. It's a journey—one that requires clarity, trust, planning, and patience. But here's the good news: if you've made it this far into the chapter, you've already taken the most important step.

You're thinking about it.

You're looking ahead, not reacting from a place of panic or burnout. You're considering how your business can outlast you—and how to make that transition work for everyone involved.

What you've learned in this chapter is that there's no single formula. There are multiple paths, multiple timelines, and multiple kinds of successors. But the common thread is intentionality. The more deliberate you are—about readiness, relationships, and pacing—the more options you'll create.

The goal isn't just to walk away from your business. It's to **walk away well.**

Whether you step out in five years or twenty, you deserve to do it with confidence, clarity, and pride in what you've built—and in who you're entrusting it to.

In the next chapter, we'll dive into the nuts and bolts: **how to structure the deal** so it works for you, your successor, and the business itself—for the long haul.

4

MAKING THE DEAL

SECTION 1: UNDERSTANDING THE STAKES

Structuring the deal is where vision meets reality. No matter how promising a potential successor may be, or how aligned both parties feel philosophically, the success of any internal succession hinges on the financial and legal architecture that supports it. This chapter is about translating intention into structure—creating a deal that is both *workable* and *durable* over time.

Unlike external buyers, internal successors often don't have access to large sums of capital. They aren't walking into your office with a check in hand; instead, they're earning their way in, typically by using the business's future profits to fund the buyout. That creates a delicate balance. You're no longer simply selling a business—you're entering into a long-term relationship where your financial future is tied to the performance of someone else.

This is the moment where many owners falter. They either demand too much upfront, killing the deal before it starts, or they give too much away too soon and find themselves stuck in a powerless position, watching someone else run their business without the security they need. A well-structured deal avoids both extremes.

Your goal is to build a deal that reflects your priorities. Maybe you're retiring but still need consistent income. Maybe you're stepping back slowly, staying involved for a few more years. Or maybe you want out, but you care deeply about your employees, your brand, and your legacy. Whatever your situation, the structure of the deal must be tailored to meet your needs—**and** to give the successor a fair and feasible path to ownership.

A strong internal succession deal should:
- Provide security and income for the seller
- Be financially viable for the buyer
- Include clear terms, milestones, and contingency plans
- Reflect mutual trust—but be formalized in legal documents, not just handshakes

This chapter will walk you through how to determine the value of your business, set up a payment structure that works, minimize tax burdens, and protect yourself if things go sideways. We'll also explore the typical timelines for internal successions and what happens if the plan doesn't go according to plan. By the end of this chapter, you'll have the tools to create a deal that isn't just fair—it's built to last.

SECTION 2: VALUATION MODELS AND DEAL STRUCTURES

Before you can structure a deal, you need to know what the business is worth—or at least agree on a number both parties can live with. Internal succession planning doesn't always begin with a formal third-party valuation, but the process must be grounded in reality. You're not selling a dream. You're selling a living, breathing enterprise with assets, liabilities, cash flow, and a track record.

There are several ways to determine value, and the method you choose may depend on the size of your business, your goals, and how much the successor can afford to pay. But just as important as valuation is **how the deal is structured**—when and how ownership transfers, what the payment terms look like, and how to manage risk for both sides.

The examples below showcase five real-world models that reflect a wide range of internal succession strategies. Each structure has unique advantages depending on the financial strength of the business, the buyer's resources, and the seller's timeline and priorities.

Approach 1: Seller's Discretionary Earnings (SDE) and Multiples

Example: Small Service Business in Portland

Business: Maple & Pine Bookkeeping

Seller: Carla Hughes (Age 61)

Buyer: Maria Rojas (Lead Bookkeeper, employed 7 years)

The business generates **$420,000 in annual revenue.** After covering expenses, Carla's **Seller's Discretionary Earnings (SDE)**—her salary plus personal perks like a car lease and phone—comes to **$140,000 per year**.

A typical small business like this might sell for **2.5 to 3x SDE**, placing the value between **$350,000 and $420,000**. Carla and Maria agree to a **$460,000** sale price—**above the standard range**—because Carla is **carrying the financing,** taking on more risk than a traditional lender would.

Deal terms:
- $20,000 down
- $3,667/month for 10 years (covering $440,000 with modest interest)
- Payments made via monthly ACH
- Carla retains co-signing rights on the business account during repayment

Ownership transfer follows a **vesting schedule:**

- Maria receives **10% equity per year**, assuming payments are current
- Full ownership transfers after 10 years
- If Maria is more than 90 days delinquent, Carla may **pause vesting, step in to stabilize operations,** and potentially **extend the term** to allow for recovery

This seller-financed, performance-based structure rewards trust and offers both flexibility and protection. It also gives Carla a retirement income stream while making ownership achievable for Maria— without the need for external financing.

Approach 2: EBITDA Multiples
(Larger or More Profitable Companies)

Example: Manufacturing Business in Dallas
Business: Lone Star Metalworks
Seller: Don Whitaker (Age 66)
Buyer: Jamal Edwards (COO, with the company 12 years)

Annual revenue is **$6 million**, with **$1.1 million in EBITDA**. A third-party valuation values the business at **$5 million** (4.5x EBITDA), accounting for customer concentration and market volatility.

Deal terms:
- $500,000 down (via SBA loan)
- $250,000/year over 7 years, paid from profits
- Don receives a **5% revenue bonus** in any year revenue exceeds $7 million
- Don retains a board advisory role with no operational authority

This structure provides a clean long-term exit while giving Jamal the ability to fund the purchase using the company's future earnings. Bonus incentives align both parties around continued growth.

Approach 3: Deferred Ownership Transfer
Example: Retail Store in Michigan
Business: Ann Arbor Cycle Co.
Seller: Dave Thompson (Age 59)
Buyer: Eli Jameson (Store Manager, working since age 19)
Annual revenue is **$280,000**, profit is **$35,000**, and the business owns **$120,000 in inventory** and **$15,000 in tools and equipment**.

Dave and Eli agree on a **$135,000 sale price**, but structure the deal as follows:

- **No down payment**
- **$1,500/month for 90 months** (7.5 years)
- **Dave retains 100% legal ownership** during this time
- **Eli takes over operations immediately**, managing staff, vendors, and customers
- **Full ownership transfers** only after all payments are completed

Legal documents include:
- A **Purchase Agreement** defining terms
- A **Management Agreement** granting Eli full operating control
- A **Buy-Sell Agreement** outlining conditions for ownership transfer
- A **Default Clause** allowing Dave to reclaim control if Eli misses more than two payments in a year

This structure is ideal when the buyer lacks capital but is trusted to run the business. It gives the seller security while providing a clear path to ownership for the buyer.

Approach 4: Partial Equity Transfer Up Front
Example: Marketing Agency in Denver
Business: Highpoint Creative
Seller: Jenna Tran (Age 55)
Buyer: Noah Bell (Senior Strategist, employed 5 years)

Annual profit is **$220,000**, with a business valuation of **$660,000** (3x profit). Noah has **$100,000** in savings and uses it to buy an initial **25% stake**.

Deal terms:
- $100,000 up front for 25% equity
- Remaining 75% purchased over 6 years through monthly payments
- Additional equity transferred at **12.5% per year**
- Performance benchmarks and job duties defined in a

Buy-In Agreement
- Jenna retains full control in Year 1 and gradually reduces her involvement

This staggered equity model gives both parties time to transition, allowing the buyer to build ownership gradually while the seller monetizes her equity over time.

Approach 5: Profit Share-Based Model
Example: Specialty Café in Oakland
Business: Brew & Bloom
Seller: Sal Ramirez (Age 62)
Buyer: Janelle Hart (Manager, employed 8 years)
The café averages **$80,000 in annual profit**, but income fluctuates seasonally. To reduce Janelle's risk, Sal proposes a **performance-based deal**.

Deal terms:
- $240,000 total purchase price (3x average profit)
- **No down payment**

- Janelle pays **50% of monthly net profits** to Sal
- **Minimum annual payment of $20,000**
- **Maximum term of 12 years** to avoid endless repayment
- Equity vests at **10% per year**, tied to payments

This structure works well for a business with **unpredictable income.** The buyer avoids fixed debt obligations, and the seller remains incentivized to help the business thrive. Both parties share the upside—and the risk.

A Note on Third-Party Valuations

Formal valuations conducted by CPAs or brokers can bring clarity and credibility to a deal—especially when multiple heirs or external parties are involved. But they also come with costs, typically between **$3,000 and $10,000.** In many small internal transitions, owners and successors choose to skip formal valuation and instead **negotiate a price based on industry norms and affordability.**

Regardless of the method used, the valuation must reflect **what the business can actually support.** A business that generates $100,000 in discretionary income cannot sustain a $1 million price tag unless the seller is willing to wait a decade or longer for payment. That's why deal structure and timeline are just as important as the final number.

SECTION 3: DECIDING ON THE PAYMENT STRUCTURE

Once you've agreed on a value for the business, the next question is: **how will the money actually change hands?** For most internal successions, the answer isn't a single wire transfer—it's a structured payment plan that unfolds over years. That structure can take many forms, and getting it right is one of the most important decisions you'll make.

Unlike external buyers—who often bring a bank loan or private equity funds to the table—internal successors usually don't have access to large pools of capital. That means the seller must decide how much risk they're willing to carry, and how to build a plan that protects their income while still being achievable for the buyer.

There's no one-size-fits-all formula, but most internal deals fall into one of a few common structures:

Option 1: Fixed Monthly Payments

The most straightforward option is a fixed monthly payment, similar to a mortgage. The buyer pays the seller the same amount each month for a set number of years, often with modest interest included.

Example:
- Sale price: $360,000
- Term: 10 years
- Monthly payment: $3,000 (including interest)

Pros:
- Predictable income for the seller
- Easy to track and enforce
- Builds a sense of discipline for the buyer

Cons:
- No flexibility if the business has a slow month or year
- May overextend the buyer if payments are too aggressive

This model works best for businesses with steady, predictable cash flow—like professional services, subscription-based businesses, or retail shops with consistent revenue.

Option 2: Profit-Based Payments

Instead of fixed amounts, the buyer pays a percentage of the business's profit (or revenue) each month or quarter. This allows payments to rise and fall with performance.

Example:

- Sale price: $300,000
- Buyer pays 50% of monthly net profit until fully paid
- Minimum annual payment: $20,000
- Maximum term: 12 years

Pros:

- More manageable for the buyer during slow periods
- Keeps seller invested in the business's success
- Incentivizes buyer to grow profitability

Cons:

- Unpredictable income for the seller
- May require financial transparency or regular CPA review
- Seller carries more risk of delayed payout

This structure is ideal when revenue is seasonal or volatile, or when the buyer is starting with little to no working capital.

Option 3: Down Payment + Installments

If the buyer has access to some capital—savings, a family loan, or a home equity line—they can make a down payment and finance the rest over time.

Example:

- Sale price: $500,000
- Down payment: $100,000
- Remaining $400,000 paid over 7 years ($4,762 month)

Pros:

- Seller gets immediate lump sum
- Buyer gains instant equity and credibility
- Can reduce the term and interest charges

Cons:

- Buyer still needs access to upfront capital
- Pressure to recoup investment quickly

This is often used when the buyer is purchasing a business already generating a strong profit, or when a partial outside loan (such as SBA) is involved.

Option 4: Vesting or Milestone-Based Payments

In some deals, payments trigger **partial equity transfers** over time—often tied to milestones such as years of service, hitting revenue targets, or completing training.

Example:
- 10% ownership vests each year for 10 years
- Buyer pays $2,500/month
- Equity is paused if buyer is more than 60 days behind

Pros:
- Prevents the seller from giving away control too soon
- Encourages long-term performance
- Makes ownership feel like something earned, not just bought

Cons:
- Can be complex to document and enforce
- Buyer may feel discouraged if they hit delays
- Valuation must account for partial transfers

This is a great option for sellers who want to retain control during the transition and for buyers who are still learning the ropes.

Option 5: Balloon Payment at the End

Another option is to keep monthly payments lower, but require a large "balloon" payment at the end—funded by a refinance, business savings, or an outside investor.

Example:
- Sale price: $400,000
- Buyer pays $2,000/month for 5 years
- At year 6, buyer owes a $280,000 balloon payment

Pros:
- Easier for buyer to manage short-term
- Seller still receives full value
- Creates time for buyer to improve business cash flow

Cons:
- Balloon payment is risky if buyer can't refinance or save
- Seller may never receive the final payout
- Requires strong legal protections

This model should be used cautiously and only when the buyer has a credible plan to handle the final payment.

Building in Flexibility

No matter which structure you choose, it's smart to include flexibility:
- **Grace periods** for temporary payment delays
- **Clawback rights** for the seller if the buyer defaults (we'll cover this in Section 6)
- **Extension clauses** that allow the buyer to stretch payments if business slows

The best deals balance **security for the seller** with **achievability for the buyer.** A payment structure that feels slightly conservative is usually better than one that assumes everything will go perfectly.

SECTION 4: TAX IMPLICATIONS AND LEGAL STRUCTURES

It's not just *what* you sell—it's *how* you sell it. The legal structure of your succession deal has serious tax consequences for both the buyer and the seller. A poorly structured agreement can create unexpected tax burdens, while a smart one can significantly reduce them.

This section won't replace your CPA or attorney, but it will give you the language and framework to ask the right questions—and avoid costly mistakes.

1. Asset Sale vs. Stock Sale

The most important distinction in business sales is whether the deal is structured as an **asset sale** or a **stock sale** (or **membership interest sale** in the case of an LLC).

- In an **asset sale**, the buyer is purchasing individual business assets—equipment, inventory, customer lists, goodwill—*but not* the business entity itself.
- In a **stock sale**, the buyer purchases the **legal entity** (corporation or LLC) that owns those assets. The business continues unchanged on paper, but with a new owner.

Most small business successions are structured as asset sales, especially when the seller is financing the deal. Asset sales are easier to understand, give the buyer a clean slate, and allow selective transfer of assets and liabilities.

Asset Sale vs. Stock Sale: Real-World Examples
Example 1: Asset Sale – Small Retail Business

Business: Sunny Trails Outdoor Gear (Sole Proprietorship)
Sale Price: $300,000
Assets Included: Inventory, equipment, customer lists, goodwill
Structure: Asset Sale

Pros for Buyer:

- Can select specific assets and exclude unwanted liabilities
- Receives a stepped-up basis in assets, allowing for depreciation deductions

Cons for Seller:

- Potential for higher tax liability due to ordinary income rates on certain assets

- Must handle the dissolution of the existing business entity

Example 2: Stock Sale – Established Corporation

Business: TechNova Solutions Inc. (C Corporation)
Sale Price: $1,000,000
Structure: Stock Sale

Pros for Seller:

- Typically taxed at long-term capital gains rates, which are lower than ordinary income rates
- Simplifies the transfer process, as the entire entity is sold

Cons for Buyer:

- Inherits all existing liabilities, including potential unknown obligations
- No step-up in asset basis, limiting future depreciation deductions

2. Tax Implications for the Seller

- In an **asset sale**, the seller typically pays **capital gains tax** on the appreciated value of the assets. Some portions—like depreciation recapture on equipment—may be taxed at **ordinary income rates**, which can be higher.
- In a **stock sale**, most of the proceeds are taxed at **long-term capital gains rates**, which are usually lower (15–20% depending on income). However, fewer small buyers are willing to accept the risk of buying the whole entity, which may carry unknown liabilities.

If you're the seller, you want as much of the sale as possible taxed as long-term capital gains—but the structure must also be acceptable to the buyer.

Seller Tax Example – Asset Sale

Seller: Linda owns a bakery
- Sale Price: $500,000
- Original Purchase Price of Assets: $200,000
- Depreciation Taken: $50,000

Adjusted Basis = $200,000 - $50,000 = $150,000
Gain = $500,000 - $150,000 = $350,000

Tax Implications:

- $50,000 (depreciation recapture) taxed at ordinary income rates
- $300,000 taxed at long-term capital gains rates

Seller Tax Example – Stock Sale

Seller: Michael owns a software company
- Sale Price: $800,000
- Original Stock Basis: $300,000

Gain = $800,000 - $300,000 = $500,000
- Entire $500,000 taxed at long-term capital gains rates

3. Tax Implications for the Buyer

- Buyers generally **prefer asset sales,** because they can **depreciate or amortize** the purchase price over time.
- In a stock sale, the buyer doesn't get the same tax benefit— since the entity continues to hold the assets at their original book value.

For internal buyers—especially employees with no external financing—an asset sale also makes it easier to wrap their heads around what they're actually buying.

Buyer Tax Example – Asset Sale

Buyer: Emma purchases a landscaping business
- Purchase Price: $400,000
- Allocated as: Equipment ($100,000), Customer List ($50,000), Goodwill ($250,000)

Tax Benefits:
- Equipment depreciated over 5–7 years
- Customer list and goodwill amortized over 15 years
- Significant deductions available to offset future income

Buyer Tax Example – Stock Sale

Buyer: Daniel buys all shares of a manufacturing company for $1.2 million

Tax Considerations:
- Cannot depreciate existing assets
- No step-up in basis for tax purposes
- May face exposure to prior liabilities and legal obligations of the business

4. Legal Structures That Support Succession

LLC (Limited Liability Company)

Example: GreenLeaf Marketing is an LLC sold internally.

Advantages:
- Flexible ownership—easy to transfer minority interests
- Pass-through taxation avoids double taxation
- Well-suited for gradual ownership transfers
- Can customize profit splits even if ownership isn't equal

S Corporation

Example: BrightStar Consulting is an S Corp being passed to a family member.

Advantages:
- Profits taxed only at the individual level
- Simpler ownership transfer than C Corps
- Restrictions: only U.S. citizens or residents may be shareholders; max 100 shareholders

C Corporation

Example: TechWorld Inc., a C Corporation sold to a team of managers.

Considerations:

- Subject to double taxation—corporate and shareholder level
- Allows for broader ownership, including other corporations
- Often used in larger companies where buyers prefer a stock purchase

5. Spreading Out the Taxes: Installment Sale Method

If you're the seller and you're receiving payments over time, you may be eligible to report the sale using the **Installment Sale Method** with the IRS. This allows you to:

- Pay taxes gradually, based on the income you receive each year
- Stay in a lower tax bracket
- Avoid a large lump-sum tax bill in the year of sale

Not all assets qualify, and some depreciation recapture must be reported in the year of sale, but for many sellers, this method offers a much smoother tax burden.

Learn more: https://irs.gov/taxtopic/tc705

Bottom Line

The structure of your deal can make a six-figure difference. Work with a tax professional and an attorney who understand **small business succession,** not just general tax law. Your future income—and peace of mind—depend on getting this right.

SECTION 5: TIMELINES AND MILESTONES

Internal succession isn't a single transaction—it's a journey. Unlike external sales, which often close in 60–90 days, internal transitions can span **5 to 20 years**. The payment timeline may be long, but the transition of leadership, responsibilities, and ownership often happens in **stages**.

That's why it's essential to define a **clear timeline** and establish **milestones** along the way. These give both parties structure, accountability, and a shared understanding of progress.

Common Succession Timelines

Here are some typical internal succession structures:

Short-Term (1–3 Years)
- Often used when the successor is highly experienced, and the seller is ready to exit quickly
- May involve a higher down payment or outside financing to accelerate the process
- Seller might stay on in a consulting role during the transition

Example: An operations manager buys out the owner of a boutique gym over 24 months, using savings and an SBA loan. The seller stays on part-time to help retain clients during the first year.

Mid-Term (5–10 Years)
- Most common structure for internal sales
- Payments are funded from the business's cash flow
- Ownership transfers gradually or vests in stages
- Seller often stays involved for 2–5 years, then steps back fully

Example: A dental practice is sold over 7 years. The associate dentist receives 10% equity per year and takes over staff management after year two. The seller retires fully in year six.

Long-Term (10–20 Years)
- Ideal when the buyer is still developing experience or the seller isn't ready to step away
- Equity transfers are slow and tied to loyalty, performance, and payments
- Often structured like an annuity for the seller

Example: A riding school owner sells to her senior instructor over 15 years. The buyer receives no equity until year five, but runs operations from year one. The deal provides steady retirement income and protects the seller from risk.

What Should Be Tracked with Milestones?

Whether you're selling in 3 years or 15, a successful internal deal uses **milestones** to stay on course. These can be written into a succession plan or buy-sell agreement and reviewed annually.

Here are some milestone categories to consider:

Ownership Benchmarks

- Transfer of initial equity percentage
- Reaching 50% or majority ownership
- Full ownership achieved after final payment

Payment Milestones

- Completion of down payment
- Annual or quarterly review of payment history
- Payment restructuring clause if revenue dips

Responsibility Shifts

- Transition of day-to-day management
- Successor begins leading staff or making hiring decisions
- Seller exits payroll, board, or operating agreement

Business Performance

- Revenue or profit targets achieved
- Client retention goals met
- Key hire or department milestone completed

Training and Development

- Successor completes training or certifications
- Attends industry conferences or joins advisory groups
- Begins representing the business in public or client settings

Sample Succession Timeline: 8-Year Deal

Year	Equity Held	Buyer Role	Seller Role	Key Milestone
1	0%	Operations Manager	Active Owner	Signs agreement, begins training
2	10%	Oversees staff, payroll	Owner reviews decisions	Receives first equity transfer
3	20%	Handles client issues directly	Reduces hours	Meets revenue goal
4	30%	Full control of day-to-day	Moves off payroll	Quarterly performance reviews only
5	50%	Majority voting rights	Board advisor	Renegotiate lease
6	70%	Leads strategic planning	Retired	Refinances balloon payment
7	90%	Full operational control	Silent partner	Expands to new market
8	100%	Full owner	None	Final payment and title transfer

Be Realistic—But Keep Moving

Internal deals are emotional and unpredictable. Life happens. A parent gets sick. A deal stalls. A recession hits. That's why having a **timeline doesn't mean being rigid**—it means being intentional.

Build in room to adjust. Agree to meet once a year (or quarterly) to review the timeline, re-evaluate expectations, and stay aligned.

SECTION 6: CONTINGENCY PLANNING

No matter how carefully you structure a deal, life doesn't always go according to plan. Internal succession deals, by their nature, take years to unfold—which means there's plenty of time for things to go sideways.

That's why every internal transition needs a **contingency plan.** These provisions protect the business, the seller's income, and the buyer's opportunity in the event of illness, underperformance, payment issues, or life events. A strong deal anticipates **what could go wrong** and lays out **what happens if it does.**

Why Contingency Clauses Matter

Without a plan for disruption, even the most promising succession can lead to confusion, resentment, or collapse. The most common points of failure include:

- The buyer falling behind on payments
- The business underperforming
- Unexpected personal events (illness, divorce, burnout)
- The seller needing to return temporarily
- A complete breakdown in communication or trust

Let's walk through specific examples to illustrate how contingency planning can protect all parties involved.

Example 1: Temporary Trouble, Deal Survives

Business: Windy Hills Dog Training
Sale Price: $320,000
Buyer: Natalie, former operations manager
Structure: $20,000 down, $2,500/month for 10 years

By year three, Natalie was consistently hitting revenue targets and had earned 30% equity. But in year four, she lost two key staff members and revenue dropped sharply. She missed two payments. Fortunately, the buy-sell agreement included a **grace clause:**

- If the buyer becomes **more than 60 days delinquent**, equity transfers pause
- If they become **90+ days delinquent,** the seller may step in temporarily
- If payments are caught up within 6 months, the buyer resumes payments and equity continues

Natalie downsized the team, focused on high-margin services, and caught up her payments within four months. The deal continued uninterrupted—just with a **pause in equity growth.** Today, she owns 70% of the business and is on track to take full ownership in year 10.

Key Takeaway: Build in room for life to happen. Don't let one bad quarter destroy a decade-long plan.

Example 2: Seller Steps Back In

Business: Brightside Family Dentistry
Sale Price: $750,000
Buyer: Tyler, a junior dentist on staff
Structure: $50,000 down, $5,000/month for 12 years

In year two, Tyler struggled to lead the team. Staff turnover increased, patient satisfaction dropped, and collections fell by 30%. The seller, Dr. Kapoor, stepped back into the business temporarily under a **performance clause** that allowed:

- The seller to **resume operational control** if revenue dropped more than 25% for three consecutive months
- Equity transfers to **freeze** until performance benchmarks were met
- A renegotiation window to adjust payments or extend the term

Dr. Kapoor returned for six months, re-hired support staff, and coached Tyler through team management. Payments resumed and equity restarts at a slower pace, extending the term by two years.

Key Takeaway: Step-in clauses aren't just about punishment—they're also about partnership. Used wisely, they can *save* a struggling buyer from failure.

Example 3: The Seller Claws Back the Business

Business: Summit Cycle & Fitness
Sale Price: $500,000
Buyer: Ryan, longtime store manager
Structure: No down payment, $3,500/month for 12 years

In year four, Ryan fell significantly behind on payments after a failed expansion. He was 5 months delinquent and not returning calls. The business began missing vendor payments, and the landlord issued a notice for lease termination.

The seller had protected herself with a **clawback clause**, which stated:

- If payments are more than **90 days late**, the seller can initiate repossession of the business
- If the buyer is **180+ days delinquent**, equity is forfeited and the deal is canceled
- A clause allowed the seller to **retain all prior payments** as liquidated damages

The seller re-entered the business, stabilized it, and sold it one year later to a new buyer. Ryan lost all equity and was released from the business.

Key Takeaway: Protect yourself with **firm legal triggers**—especially when no down payment is involved.

Example 4: A Cautionary Tale – No Contingencies, Deal Collapses

Business: Artisan Frame Studio
Sale Price: $280,000
Buyer: Anna, apprentice framer
Structure: $1,500/month for 15 years; no down payment

There was **no written agreement.** Equity was to be "given over time" but not documented. Payments were made irregularly. When Anna missed several payments during a personal health crisis, the seller became angry and tried to revoke the arrangement.

With no contract, both parties claimed ownership. Staff left. Revenue collapsed. The business closed in year five. Neither side recovered their investment.

Key Takeaway: No matter how close you are, put everything in writing. Friendship is not a legal structure.

Elements of a Strong Contingency Plan

A well-drafted agreement should include:

- **Grace Periods:** Allow short-term delays without default
- **Performance Triggers:** If revenue or profit drops, pause equity and initiate review
- **Step-In Clauses:** Allow seller to resume partial or full control temporarily
- **Clawback Rights:** Give seller the ability to reclaim the business if payments stop or trust breaks down
- **Extension Options:** Let buyer extend the term in hard times rather than default
- **Buyout or Exit Clauses:** Define what happens if either party wants out early
- **Liquidated Damages:** Predefined financial consequences if the deal collapses

Don't Wait for the Storm

If you think you'll "figure it out later," you won't. Create clear rules while everyone is optimistic and cooperative. You're not just planning for worst-case scenarios—you're giving the deal a **real chance to survive them.**

SECTION 7: COMMUNICATION AND TRANSPARENCY

Internal successions don't just happen on paper—they happen in the workplace, in the community, and in the minds of your team and clients. That means the *way* you communicate your succession plan is just as important as the plan itself.

Handled well, transparency can build confidence, inspire loyalty, and make the transition feel natural. Handled poorly—or not at all—it can create confusion, rumors, or even trigger turnover.

This section explores how and when to communicate your plan to employees, clients, vendors, and other stakeholders.

The Most Common Mistake: Saying Too Much or Too Little

Many business owners swing to one of two extremes:

- **They tell everyone too early**, before the deal is formalized or stable—creating anxiety and instability.
- **They tell no one until the very end**, leading to confusion, gossip, and resistance.

The best approach is to treat succession as a **process**, not an announcement. Communicate in **stages**, using a "need-to-know-when-they-need-to-know" mindset—while keeping tone, timing, and message aligned with reality.

Stage 1: Early Confidential Planning

In the first year or two of internal succession discussions, communication should be **highly limited:**

- The buyer and seller should **document confidentiality** in writing
- Avoid sharing details with staff or clients until a preliminary agreement is in place
- Begin coaching or mentoring quietly, without fanfare
- This prevents destabilizing the business if the plan changes or falls through.

Stage 2: Internal Communication with Staff

Once the agreement is formalized and key milestones are underway, **loop in your team**—starting with leadership, then gradually informing the full staff.

Best Practices:

- Present the change as **planned and strategic,** not reactive
- Emphasize **continuity:** the business will still operate under the same values and mission
- Reassure staff that their roles, pay, and culture are not threatened
- Highlight the successor's qualifications and long-standing relationship with the company

Sample Script for Team Announcement:

"As part of our long-term vision, I've been working on a gradual transition plan with [Buyer's Name], who many of you already know and respect. Over the next few years, they'll be stepping into more leadership, while I shift into a mentorship role. This change won't impact your jobs—our mission, culture, and client service will remain just as strong."

Stage 3: Client and Vendor Communication

Once the buyer has begun leading operations—or at least has a visible presence—begin gradually **introducing them to clients and vendors as a key decision-maker.**

Avoid: Announcing a sale with "effective immediately" language
Do: Talk about the transition as something that is **planned, phased, and built on trust**

Key talking points:
- "We're planning for the future while protecting the values that got us here."
- "You'll still see me around, but [Buyer's Name] is taking on more responsibility to ensure long-term continuity."
- "Nothing is changing about how we serve you—we're simply evolving for the next chapter."

Stage 4: Public Announcement (Optional)

If your business has a public-facing brand, media presence, or community visibility, you may choose to make a **formal public announcement** once the majority of ownership has transferred.

This can include:
- A press release

- A blog post or social media campaign
- A note on your website introducing the new owner
- A client appreciation event

Public messaging should focus on the **legacy** of the business and your confidence in the next generation of leadership.

Keep Communicating During the Transition

The most successful transitions don't just have one "big announcement." They have **consistent, clear communication** over time. Schedule periodic updates:

- Team meetings to check in on morale and address questions
- One-on-one check-ins with key staff or clients
- Annual reviews of the transition plan

Even something as simple as a staff email every quarter updating progress can make everyone feel informed and reassured.

Final Tip: Align Words with Reality

If the seller is still making all the decisions behind the scenes, don't tell the team the buyer is "now in charge." That creates confusion and undermines credibility. Make sure what you **say publicly** matches what's **happening operationally.**

Succession is part communication, part choreography. Don't just plan the handoff—plan how you'll talk about it, too.

SECTION 8: CASE STUDY- STRUCTURING A WIN-WIN

Sometimes the best way to understand how all the moving parts of an internal succession come together is to see it in action. The following is a **composite case study**—based on real-world patterns and adapted from multiple successful transitions. It walks through a full internal sale, highlighting the valuation, deal structure, timeline, challenges, and outcome.

Business Profile: Meadow Creek Physical Therapy

- **Location:** Asheville, North Carolina
- **Annual Revenue:** $950,000
- **Net Profit:** $180,000
- **Staff:** 6 employees (3 therapists, 3 administrative)
- **Owner:** Carolyn Becker (age 60)
- **Successor:** James Carter (lead therapist, with the company for 9 years)

Stage 1: Identifying the Successor

Carolyn wanted to retire without selling to a corporate chain. She hoped to keep the practice personal, ethical, and rooted in the community. James had been her lead therapist for nearly a decade, and while he wasn't flashy, he was steady, trustworthy, and beloved by patients and staff.

They began with a simple conversation. James admitted he'd love to own the practice—but he was skeptical it could ever happen.

"I don't own a house. I rent a two-bedroom apartment downtown. My credit is fine—not great—and I only have about $10,000 in savings. No bank's going to give me a loan."

He was right. The **SBA isn't typically excited about borrowers who rent, have average credit, and no collateral.** But Carolyn didn't see James as a credit score—she saw him as the future of the business.

Stage 2: Valuation and Deal Structure

After reviewing the books and speaking to a CPA, they settled on a valuation of **$540,000**, which was about **3x net profit**.

Normally, a deal of this size might have sold for 2.5x earnings—but Carolyn was **carrying the note,** taking on all the financial risk. That **warrants a higher multiple,** especially since James wasn't using a bank or outside lender.

They agreed to:

- **$2,500 down payment** (just 25% of James's savings—he kept a cushion for emergencies)
- **$4,000/month for 10 years**, including modest interest
- Payments went directly to Carolyn as retirement income
- **10% equity transferred annually**, provided payments were current
- **Clawback clause:** if payments fell 90+ days behind or revenue dropped 25%, Carolyn could resume control

Stage 3: Legal and Tax Planning

An attorney helped them draft:

- A **Buy-Sell Agreement** with annual vesting tied to payment compliance
- A **Promissory Note** with a default clause and interest schedule
- A **Management Agreement** granting James operational control from Day 1
- An **asset sale structure**, allowing James to depreciate the goodwill, customer lists, and equipment

Carolyn used the **Installment Sale Method** to spread her tax burden over the 10 years of payments, keeping her in a lower tax bracket during retirement.

Stage 4: Communicating the Transition

They waited until the third month of payments to tell the staff. Carolyn led with reassurance:

"I'm not going anywhere overnight. James and I have mapped out a long-term plan, and you're going to see him take on more and more over time."

Clients were introduced to James as co-owner by year two. Carolyn stayed involved in back-end operations but started cutting back her clinic days.

Stage 5: Setbacks and Adjustments

In year three, a nearby orthopedic center opened and lured away one of their part-time therapists. Revenues dipped by 18% over two quarters. James met with Carolyn, shared a recovery plan, and trimmed non-essential marketing expenses.

Carolyn granted a **grace period** for payments and paused equity transfer for six months. They later **extended the agreement by 10 months** to make up for the lost time. By year four, revenue had stabilized, and James was back on schedule.

Stage 6: Final Ownership Transfer

By year ten:

- James had made every payment
- Carolyn had earned nearly $80,000 in interest
- James owned 100% of the business
- Carolyn hosted a retirement celebration for clients and staff and handed over the clinic keys

Today, James runs Meadow Creek independently. He still rents his apartment—but he owns a thriving business and recently hired a second full-time therapist. Carolyn still visits occasionally—but only as a patient.

Lessons from Meadow Creek

1. Your buyer doesn't have to be rich to be the right person.
2. Carrying the financing gives you control—and justifies a higher sale price.
3. Small down payments are okay if the structure is strong.
4. Let the buyer keep an emergency fund.
5. Document protections that help the deal survive setbacks.
6. A modest, consistent buyer can outperform a flashy one.

SECTION 9: WRAP-UP—CUSTOMIZING THE FRAMEWORK

There's no single way to structure an internal succession—and that's exactly the point.

This chapter has laid out a variety of tools: valuation methods, payment structures, tax strategies, legal protections, timelines, and communication plans. But what matters most isn't choosing the "right" structure—it's building the one that fits **your business, your successor, and your goals.**

Maybe your successor is buying in slowly with sweat equity. Maybe they're starting with a down payment and taking over quickly. Maybe you're offering a long-term annuity because they can't get outside financing. Every deal is different. The key is to stay realistic, protect both sides, and plan for what could go wrong—so you're positioned to ride it out when it does.

A well-designed internal succession is more than a financial transaction. It's a trust-based handoff that preserves the values you've built, protects your legacy, and gives the next generation a foundation to grow from. You're not just passing on a business. You're passing on an identity, a way of doing things, a reputation in your community.

So take the time to do it right. Invest in clarity. Be honest about risk. Get it in writing.

And remember: The goal isn't just to sell your business. The goal is to **leave it standing stronger than when you started.**

5

FINANCING
THE DEAL

SECTION 1: CREATIVE FINANCING IS THE NORM

In a traditional business sale, the buyer walks in with a briefcase full of cash—or more likely, a bank loan. But internal successions aren't traditional. In fact, they almost always require **nontraditional financing,** especially when the buyer is someone who wouldn't otherwise qualify for a loan.

This chapter is for those people.

The buyer might be:

- A longtime employee who **rents an apartment**, not owns a home
- Someone with a **liberal arts degree** and no formal business education
- A person with **average credit**, no savings, and no experience running a company
- Someone who's never thought of themselves as an "entrepreneur"—but has already been *acting like one* for years on the job

And here's the good news: those people can—and do—buy businesses all the time. Internal succession makes it possible.

These deals aren't built on perfect résumés or 800 credit scores. They're built on:

- Long-term working relationships
- Trust
- Deep operational knowledge of the business
- And, above all, **creatively structured financing**

If you're selling, **this chapter will help you understand** how to make the numbers work—even if your buyer doesn't come in with cash or collateral. If you're buying, this chapter will show you how to acquire a business without winning the lottery first.

Internal successions work because the seller and buyer can **custom-build a deal around reality,** not around what a traditional lender says is possible. Sometimes that means the seller accepts a lower price in exchange for a slow, secure wind-down. Other times, it means the seller charges a premium—because they're taking all the risk, and they deserve to be compensated for it.

This chapter will walk you through both paths. You'll see how these deals are funded in the real world—not just in theory. Because when the right successor meets the right structure, the money almost always finds a way to follow.

SECTION 2: EXPLORING SBA LOANS: OPPORTUNITIES AND CHALLENGES

For many aspiring business owners, the SBA 7(a) loan program seems like the golden ticket. It offers long repayment terms, relatively low interest rates, and is specifically designed to help people acquire small businesses. It sounds like the perfect solution—and for a small number of well-qualified buyers, it can be.

But for the vast majority of internal successors, **SBA loans aren't the answer.** The program has strict requirements that rule out many of the people best suited to take over a small business from the inside: renters, people with average credit, people without a business degree, or people who've never owned a company before.

This section breaks down what an SBA loan actually is, who's eligible, and what happens when things go wrong—plus three real-world examples of deals that did (and didn't) involve SBA funding.

What Is an SBA 7(a) Loan?

The SBA 7(a) loan is the most popular loan guaranteed by the U.S. Small Business Administration. It can be used for working capital, real estate, equipment, or—to our focus here—**purchasing an existing business.**

Key features:
- **Loan Amounts:** Up to $5 million
- **Repayment Terms:** Up to 10 years for business acquisitions
- **Interest Rates:** Negotiated between the borrower and the lender, but capped by SBA guidelines
- **Guarantee:** SBA backs up to 85% of the loan (reducing risk for the lender)

Who Is the "Lender" in an SBA Loan?

One common misunderstanding is that the SBA gives you the money. It doesn't.

SBA loans are issued by **banks, credit unions, and other approved lenders**—not by the federal government itself. The SBA simply **guarantees part of the loan,** which makes the lender more willing to take the risk.

So when we say the interest rate is negotiated between the borrower and the lender, we're talking about:
- A **traditional bank**
- A **credit union**
- Or a **specialized community lender** like a CDFI (Community Development Financial Institution)

The SBA steps in only if the borrower defaults and the lender can't recover the loaned amount through collateral.

Real-World Examples

Example 1: Successful SBA Loan Acquisition

Emily had worked at a local bakery for over ten years. When the owner decided to retire, she expressed interest in buying the business. Though her credit was average and her savings modest, her deep operational experience and strong client relationships impressed the lender. She provided a 10% down payment—funded through savings and a small family gift—and secured an SBA loan for the rest. The loan closed within 90 days, and the seller received their money in full.

Example 2: SBA Loan + Seller Financing Hybrid

Carlos, a landscaping manager, tried to buy the business he helped build. He secured an SBA loan for 80% of the purchase price, but the lender required additional security and wouldn't fund the full amount. The seller agreed to carry the remaining 20% as a secondary loan. This made the deal bankable without requiring Carlos to contribute more cash up front. The seller received most of their money at closing and the rest over three years.

Example 3: SBA Denial Leads to Seller Financing

Jasmine managed a boutique fitness studio and hoped to take over when the owner moved out of state. She applied for an SBA loan, but her application was denied—her credit score was in the low 600s, she rented her apartment, and she lacked personal assets. Rather than give up, she and the seller structured a deal using seller financing: no down payment, $3,000/month for eight years. Jasmine now runs the business and has already paid off over a third of the note.

Why Sellers Love SBA Loans

From the seller's perspective, SBA deals are ideal:
- They get **all their money up front**, at closing
- They're not carrying any financing risk
- They don't have to manage payments or worry about default

It's a clean, one-time transaction—similar to selling a house.

But it only works **if the buyer qualifies,** and in many internal transitions, the buyer doesn't.

What Happens if the Buyer Defaults on an SBA Loan?

If the business fails and the buyer can't repay the loan:

1. **The lender attempts to collect** by seizing business assets and any personal collateral.
2. **The SBA pays the lender back** for the guaranteed portion of the loan (usually 75–85%).
3. **The buyer is still responsible** for the unpaid amount and must repay the SBA. They can't walk away from the debt.
4. **The seller is not liable,** unless they committed fraud or misrepresentation.

However, if the seller carried a **secondary loan (a "seller note") behind the SBA loan,** the SBA may restrict repayment of that seller note until the primary loan is repaid or current.

Bottom Line

SBA loans can work beautifully—but usually only for buyers who have:
- Good credit
- Some personal savings
- Relevant experience
- And ideally, some assets the lender can seize if things go wrong

If that's not your buyer, all is not lost. The next section explores **why seller financing is the most common solution for internal succession—** and why it often results in better long-term outcomes for both parties.

SECTION 3: SELLER FINANCING: HOW AND WHY IT WORKS

When SBA loans don't pan out—and they often don't—the most common solution is **seller financing.**

In a seller-financed deal, the seller doesn't get all their money up front. Instead, the buyer pays over time, usually through monthly installments funded by the business itself. In many internal successions, this is the **only way** a deal gets done.

And surprisingly? It often works better for both sides.

Why Seller Financing Makes Sense

For the buyer, seller financing makes business ownership possible— even if they:

- Rent their apartment
- Have average credit
- Don't have savings or a 20% down payment
- Never went to business school
- Have never owned a company before

Traditional lenders would say no to this buyer. But the seller knows this person. They've worked together for years. The buyer already understands the business, the customers, the team. They just don't have a checkbook big enough to satisfy a bank.

For the seller, carrying the note opens the door to a higher sale price. Why? Because they're taking the risk—and risk deserves a premium.

Let's say your business normally sells for 2.5x earnings. If you're offering seller financing and shouldering all the uncertainty, you can often justify a **3x multiple or higher**. You're not just selling the business—you're making ownership *possible*. That creates value.

Typical Seller Financing Terms

While every deal is different, here's what a standard seller-financed deal might look like:

- **Down Payment:** 0–10%
- **Term Length:** 5 to 15 years
- **Interest Rate:** 5%–8% (sometimes lower for employee deals)
- **Monthly Payment:** Fixed, or tied to business performance
- **Equity Transfer:** Vested gradually (e.g., 10% per year) or delayed until full payment

The buyer runs the business. The seller receives steady income—often enough to fund retirement. And both sides are aligned: the better the business performs, the faster and more securely the seller gets paid.

Real-World Examples

Example 1: Seller Financing with No Down Payment

Tomas had worked at a family-owned print shop since he was 21. At 42, he knew every aspect of the business—but had no college degree, no real savings, and a 660 credit score. The owner offered to sell him the business for **$320,000**, based on **$110,000 in SDE multiplied by 2.9x**, factoring in consistent revenue and a loyal client base.

Tomas had $4,000 in the bank. No SBA lender would take the deal.

They structured a 10-year seller-financed agreement:
- $0 down
- $3,395/month
- 6% interest
- Equity vested 10% per year
- If Tomas defaulted by 90+ days, the seller had the right to reclaim the business

Here's how it works:
- $320,000 loan
- 10-year term
- 6% annual interest
- Monthly payment: **$3,395.06**

- Total paid over 10 years: **$407,407**, including approximately **$87,407 in interest**

Tomas made every payment, doubled the revenue, and paid off the loan slightly ahead of schedule in year nine.

Example 2: Partial Ownership with Seller Financing

Alyssa had worked as the assistant director at a children's art studio for eight years. When the owner offered to sell, they agreed on a business valuation of **$180,000**, based on **$60,000/year in SDE** and a **3x multiple**. The owner priced the deal slightly below market to reflect Alyssa's loyalty and to ensure the studio would remain true to its mission.

They structured a phased seller-financed deal:
- $5,000 down payment, leaving $175,000 financed
- 5-year term at 5% interest
- Monthly payments of **$3,000**
- Alyssa received 25% equity up front, then earned 15% more each year as long as payments were current
- Full ownership transferred once the final payment was made

Here's how it works:
- $175,000 loan
- 5-year term
- 5% annual interest
- Monthly payment: **$3,000**
- After 60 payments, Alyssa owed a **final balloon payment of $9,850** to settle the balance
- Total paid: $189,850, including $14,850 in interest

Alyssa expanded programming and introduced birthday parties, boosting annual revenue. The seller continues to receive monthly income—and occasionally guest-teaches a spring clay class.

Example 3: Performance-Based Seller Financing

Devon, a stable manager at a small equestrian facility, had managed operations for 12 years. The owner offered to sell him the business for **$600,000**, based on a blended valuation of **$250,000 in assets (horses, equipment, tack)** plus **$70,000/year in SDE**, using a **2.5x multiple** on the earnings portion.

Devon couldn't get financing and had no down payment, so they structured a performance-based deal:
- $0 down
- $6,663/month
- 6% interest
- 10-year term
- Ownership transferred in full at the end of the term

Here's how it works:
- $600,000 loan
- 10-year term
- 6% annual interest
- Monthly payment: **$6,662.74**
- Total paid over 10 years: **$799,528.80**, including **$199,528 in interest**

Devon adjusted staffing in the off-season and focused on higher-margin training and lesson programs. He's now in year six of the deal and slightly ahead on payments.

Seller Protections

Seller financing isn't a free-for-all. A well-written agreement includes:
- **Personal guarantees**
- **Default clauses and grace periods**
- **Step-in rights** if the buyer mismanages the business
- **Clawback provisions** to reclaim ownership if payments stop
- **Performance benchmarks** for equity transfers

You're not just handing over the business—you're building a contract that gives you legal protection and reliable income.

Why This Is the Default Path in Internal Succession

It's personal. It's flexible. It's realistic.

Seller financing works because it's built on something banks can't see: **relationships, trust, and time.**

Up next, we'll explore some **hybrid models**—creative combinations of seller notes, equity buy-ins, and profit-sharing that can unlock even more options.

SECTION 4: HYBRID MODELS

Not every internal succession deal is 100% seller-financed—or completely reliant on an SBA loan. Many of the most successful transitions fall somewhere in the middle: **hybrid models** that combine financing sources or ownership strategies to make the numbers work.

These flexible structures allow the buyer and seller to balance **cash, risk, and control**—while still keeping the deal achievable and fair.

Common Hybrid Approaches
1. SBA Loan + Seller Financing

Business: Red Maple Accounting
Location: Rochester, New York
Valuation: $500,000

After working at Red Maple Accounting for 12 years, **Latoya**, a senior bookkeeper, was offered the opportunity to buy the firm when the owner retired. She qualified for an SBA loan, but the bank would only lend $400,000. To make the deal work, the seller carried a note for the remaining $100,000, structured over five years at 5% interest.

A clause in the agreement stated that if Latoya fell behind on payments for more than 60 days, the seller could **pause equity transfer** and **temporarily resume operational oversight** until the deal stabilized. If payments were missed for 90+ days, a **clawback clause** allowed the seller to reclaim partial ownership.

This hybrid allowed Latoya to take over with confidence, while giving the seller peace of mind and a continued financial return.

2. Cash Buy-In + Seller Financing

Business: Tiny Trails Preschool
Location: Bend, Oregon
Valuation: $250,000

Marcus, the assistant director, had saved $25,000 over six years and was ready to take the next step. The school's founder wanted to retire but needed income from the business to fund her move. They structured a hybrid deal:

- Marcus paid **$25,000 down**
- Seller financed the remaining **$225,000** over seven years at 6% interest
- Marcus received **25% equity at closing**, and the remainder would vest annually based on payment compliance

The contract included **performance benchmarks** for enrollment and revenue. If Marcus missed more than two payments in a year or if enrollment fell below a set threshold, the seller could **pause the deal, step back in temporarily,** or extend the payment timeline.

This structure allowed Marcus to take ownership gradually while ensuring the business stayed financially healthy.

3. Earn-In Model

Business: The Canopy Café
Location: Missoula, Montana
Valuation: $300,000

Janelle, a front-of-house manager with no capital but a strong work ethic, had been the heart of The Canopy Café for years. The retiring owner didn't want to lose the community she had built—but also couldn't afford to give the business away.

They agreed to an **earn-in deal:**

- Janelle received **10% equity immediately**
- She earned an additional **10% equity per year** by maintaining labor costs, handling payroll, and growing event bookings
- Instead of a salary increase, she took a small reduction to fund the transition
- The business remained in the seller's name until the final year, when full equity transferred

To protect the seller, the agreement included a **clawback provision:** if Janelle left or performance targets were missed for more than two quarters, equity transfer would pause and ownership would revert partially or fully to the seller.

This model worked because it aligned their goals—Janelle had a clear path to ownership, and the seller could step away slowly with confidence.

4. Profit-Sharing + Buyout

Business: Park & Ride Bicycle Repair
Location: Madison, Wisconsin
Valuation: $450,000

Evan, the lead mechanic and shop manager, had no savings or access to financing—but was already running the day-to-day operations. The owner proposed a deal based on performance:

- Evan received **25% of net annual profit**
- That profit share was applied toward the **eventual purchase of the business**
- The first two years were purely profit-share; by year three, the business would be formally revalued, and a 7-year seller-financed buyout would begin
- If Evan hit revenue targets, 10% equity would be transferred annually

To protect the seller, the contract included a **performance review every six months.** If profits fell below a specified threshold or if customer satisfaction dropped significantly, the seller could **pause the equity plan, step back in temporarily, or trigger a buyback clause.**

This arrangement allowed Evan to build toward ownership without upfront capital—while allowing the seller to exit on a rolling, data-driven timeline.

Why Hybrid Models Work

They're custom-built. Each party brings something to the table:
- The buyer brings effort, sweat equity, and operational experience
- The seller brings flexibility, financial leverage, and mentorship
- The business provides the cash flow to make the transition work over time
- Hybrid models are especially helpful when:
- The buyer **has some money,** but not enough
- The seller **wants some cash up front,** but is open to sharing risk
- There's **trust,** but both sides want **legal structure and protection**

Bottom Line

Hybrid models let you **bridge the gap** between what a buyer can afford and what a seller needs. And they don't require blind trust— just clear agreements, regular reviews, and smart exit clauses. These structures can feel more like a **partnership than a transaction**—which is exactly what internal succession is at its best.

SECTION 5: USING BUSINESS PROFITS TO FUND THE BUYOUT

In most internal successions, the buyer isn't reaching into their own pocket to make payments—they're using the business itself to generate the cash. And when the business is healthy and well-run, this can be a win for both sides.

This structure is especially common when:
- The buyer has little or no savings
- The seller is open to monthly payments over time
- The business already produces consistent, positive cash flow

Done well, the business funds the purchase **without harming operations**—but only if payments are realistic and the transition is carefully structured.

How It Works

In a profit-funded deal:

- The seller finances the purchase
- The buyer takes over day-to-day operations
- Monthly payments to the seller come **directly from business income,** not personal funds
- The deal is structured around the business's actual cash flow

The key is to **analyze the business's financials honestly** and build a payment plan the company can sustain. If monthly payments are too aggressive, the business may become unstable—hurting both parties.

Real-World Examples

Example #1: Horizon Pool Services – Mesa, Arizona

Valuation: $360,000
Buyer: Tyler (Operations Manager)
Seller: Greg (Founder)
Business Type: Pool cleaning and repair service
Valuation Basis: $120,000/year in SDE × 3.0 multiple

Tyler had managed Horizon Pool Services for five years. When Greg decided to retire, they structured the following deal:

- $0 down
- **$3,818/month** for 10 years at 5% interest
- Equity vested **10% per year** based on payment compliance
- Payments made entirely from business profits

Seller protections:

- **Clawback clause:** triggered if payments are 90+ days late
- **Performance clause:** equity transfer pauses if net profit drops more than 20% for two consecutive quarters
- **Semiannual financial reviews**

Here's how it works:

- Total paid over 10 years: **$458,203.03**
- Total interest: **$98,203.03**

Tyler acquired the business without using personal savings. Greg retired with peace of mind and a steady income stream backed by a business he built.

Example #2: Sunset Event Rentals – Sacramento, California

Valuation: $400,000
Buyer: Simone (Logistics Manager)
Seller: Daryl (Owner)
Business Type: Event equipment rentals (tents, tables, AV)
Valuation Basis: $100,000/year in SDE × **4.0 multiple**
(*Seller charged a premium for carrying the financing risk*)

Simone had worked at Sunset for eight years. She didn't have access to financing but knew the business inside and out. Daryl agreed to carry the full note himself, in exchange for a higher sale price.

- $0 down
- **$4,440.82/month** for 10 years at 6% interest
- **100% ownership transferred only after the final payment was made**
- Simone took over operations immediately but legal ownership remained with Daryl until the loan was paid in full

Seller protections:

- **Step-in clause:** Daryl could resume day-to-day control if Simone missed more than one payment
- **Reversion clause:** If the business dropped below 75% of baseline revenue for two quarters, he could pause or restructure the deal
- **Personal guarantee** signed by Simone

Here's how it works:
- Total paid over 10 years: **$532,898.41**
- Total interest: **$132,898.41**

Simone earned ownership without needing upfront capital. Daryl walked away with a higher long-term return than he would have received from a cash buyer—and retained full ownership as security until the final dollar was paid.

Example #3: Blue Paw Grooming Studio – Ann Arbor, Michigan
Valuation: $250,000
Buyer: Andre (Senior Groomer)
Seller: Brenda (Founder)
Business Type: Pet grooming and boarding
Valuation Basis: $85,000/year in SDE × 2.9 multiple

Andre had a great rapport with clients and deep operational experience. Brenda wanted to retire but also ensure continuity for her loyal customers.They structured the deal as:

- $0 down
- **$2,651.64/month** for 10 years at 5% interest
- Equity vested **gradually**, tied to client retention and year-over-year revenue growth
- Monthly payments came directly from Blue Paw's operating income

Seller protections:
- **Grace clause:** one missed payment per year allowed without penalty
- **Clawback clause:** all transferred equity would revert if Andre missed three payments in a rolling 12-month period
- **Consulting agreement:** Brenda stayed involved for 18 months, with the right to pause equity transfer if customer retention dropped below 80%

Here's how it works:
- Total paid over 10 years: **$318,196.55**
- Total interest: **$68,196.55**

Andre successfully transitioned into full ownership while continuing to grow the business. Brenda stayed involved just long enough to ensure her legacy—and her retirement—were secure.

Why This Works

This model works because:
- It allows a buyer with **no savings or loan access** to buy a business
- It gives the seller **predictable monthly income**—often more than they'd earn if they sold outright
- The business itself **funds the transition**, making the deal feasible without outside capital
- But it only works if both sides are practical:
- Set payments at a level the business can support
- Include **clawbacks, step-in rights, and pause clauses**
- Build in regular check-ins to spot problems early

SECTION 6: WHEN THE SELLER NEEDS MORE UP FRONT

Not every seller is in a position to wait ten years for a full payout. Some need **cash up front**—to pay off debt, relocate, fund another venture, or simply feel secure about stepping away.

Internal successors often can't write a big check, but that doesn't mean the deal has to fall apart. There are creative ways to meet the seller's need for liquidity while keeping the deal achievable for the buyer.

Strategy 1: Partial SBA Loan for Early Liquidity
Business: Bella Bloom Florals

Location: Napa, California
Seller: Rosa (Owner and Founder)
Buyer: Lily (Lead Designer)
Business Type: Boutique florist and event design studio
Valuation: $400,000, based on $100,000/year SDE and a 4x multiple

Rosa needed $100,000 up front to pay off personal debt. Lily didn't have savings, but she qualified for an SBA loan covering the first $100,000 based on her credit and the business's strong track record.

Deal structure:
- **$100,000 SBA loan** paid to Rosa at closing
- **Remaining $300,000** seller-financed over 7 years at 6% interest
- Monthly payment to Rosa: **$4,382.57**
- Equity vested 15% per year over the life of the loan

Seller protections:
- **Step-in clause**: Rosa could temporarily resume operations if two payments were missed
- **Clawback clause:** equity transfer paused if revenue declined more than 25% for two consecutive quarters
- **Six-month reviews** built into the contract

Rosa got the early payout she needed, and Lily was able to take over the business she loved—without needing to personally invest upfront capital beyond the SBA loan.

Strategy 2: Modest Business, Discounted Deal
Business: The Cookie Counter
Location: Tempe, Arizona
Seller: Brian (Founder and Baker)
Buyer: Caleb (Kitchen Manager)
Business Type: Small-batch bakery and café

Valuation (Fair Market): $200,000
Agreed Sale Price: $180,000
(*Seller accepted a $20,000 discount in exchange for a larger up-front payment and shorter financing timeline.*)

Brian wanted a clean exit and didn't want to wait a decade for full repayment. Caleb had saved $30,000 from his years at the bakery and was eager to step up.

Deal structure:

- **$30,000 down payment** at closing
- **$150,000 seller-financed** over 5 years at 5% interest
- Monthly payment: **$2,830.69**
- Equity vested at 20% per year, with full ownership transferring at the end of the term

Seller protections:

- **Grace clause:** one missed payment allowed per year without penalty
- **Step-in clause:** Brian could temporarily resume operations if performance fell below key benchmarks
- **Key-person insurance:** Policy on Caleb with Brian named as beneficiary

Brian got most of his cash sooner and reduced long-term risk. Caleb got a fair deal and the opportunity to build on the bakery's strong local following.

Strategy 3: Balloon Payment at the End

Business: Urban Paw Supply Co.
Location: Denver, Colorado
Seller: Marianne (Owner)
Buyer: Jake (Inventory and Marketing Lead)
Business Type: Pet supply store with grooming services and online sales
Valuation: $325,000, based on $90,000/year in SDE and a 3.6x multiple

Jake had vision and drive—but no savings. He and Marianne created a deal that minimized his early financial burden while ensuring she eventually received the full purchase amount.

Deal structure:
- $0 down
- **$3,180.13/month** for 7 years (on $225,000 at 5% interest)
- **$100,000 balloon payment due at the start of year 8**
- Full equity transferred once the balloon payment was made

Why it worked:
Jake had a concrete plan to increase profitability by:
- Launching an e-commerce platform for recurring pet food delivery
- Adding a self-service dog wash station
- Expanding into branded accessories and event sponsorships

He projected that profits would double within five years—making the balloon payment realistic through retained earnings or future financing.

Seller protections:
- **Clawback clause:** if Jake missed more than two monthly payments or defaulted on the balloon, ownership reverted
- **Semiannual performance reviews**
- **Pause clause** tied to client retention and profit benchmarks

Jake gained time to build revenue and prepare for the balloon, while Marianne retained full ownership as security until the final payment was made.

Protecting the Seller When More Cash Is Needed
Whenever a seller takes less up front than they'd prefer, strong legal guardrails are essential:
- **Clawback clauses** for missed payments or underperformance
- **Balloon payment schedules** with specific deadlines and triggers
- **Step-in rights** to allow temporary operational control

- **Personal guarantees** or liens on business assets
- **Life and disability insurance** to mitigate buyer risk

Even if full payment isn't possible at closing, **partial liquidity plus strong protections** can give sellers the confidence to move forward— and give buyers the chance to build their future.

SECTION 7: PROTECTING THE SELLER

UCC Filings and Key Man Insurance: Two Often-Overlooked Tools

When structuring an internal succession deal, especially one involving seller financing or installment payments, two tools can help protect both parties and reduce risk: the **UCC-1 filing** and **key man insurance.**

What is a UCC Filing and Why Does It Matter?

A **UCC-1 filing** (Uniform Commercial Code Form 1) is a public legal notice that a creditor (in this case, often the exiting owner) has a security interest in the debtor's assets (usually the business). Think of it like a lien. It doesn't give you ownership of the business, but it puts your claim **on record**—which is especially important if the buyer defaults.

Without a UCC-1 in place, you're simply an unsecured creditor. If the business fails, you get in line with everyone else. With a UCC-1, you've secured your interest and have priority over other unsecured claims.

How to file one:

- UCC filings are typically done with the **Secretary of State** in the state where the business is organized.
- The form is often simple: it lists the debtor, the secured party, and a description of the collateral (usually "all business assets").
- Filing fees are low (often $10–$30), and many states allow online filing.

TIP: Work with an attorney to draft the proper language in your financing documents that gives you the right to file the UCC. Then file it the same day the sale closes.

What is Key Man Insurance?

Key man insurance (also called "key person insurance") is a life insurance policy taken out on a critical individual in the business—usually the owner, founder, or, in this case, the buyer or successor.

In the context of internal succession, this policy is often structured so that the **seller is the beneficiary.** If the successor dies unexpectedly before completing the buyout, the policy pays the remaining balance of the deal.

This protects:
- The seller (so they still get paid),
- The buyer's family (so they're not left with a debt), and
- The business (which can avoid being pulled apart or liquidated to settle obligations).

How to set it up:
- The business or seller takes out a term life policy on the successor.
- Coverage should match or exceed the total remaining obligation on the deal.
- The seller or original owner is named as the beneficiary.

TIP: If you're the seller and financing a large portion of the deal, **requiring a key man policy as a condition of sale** is a smart move.

SECTION 8: CLOSING THOUGHTS—STRUCTURE OVER CASH

Internal succession is rarely about the money up front. It's about the plan.

Most internal buyers can't walk into a bank and walk out with a check. They don't have wealthy relatives, massive savings, or commercial real estate to pledge as collateral. But they know the business. They've earned trust. They're willing to work hard, take risks, and grow into ownership.

And that's why **structure matters more than capital.**

There's no one-size-fits-all model. Some deals are pure seller-financing. Others combine SBA loans, down payments, profit sharing, and balloon notes. Some include vesting. Others transfer ownership in full once the final payment clears.

What matters is that the structure:
- Aligns the incentives of buyer and seller
- Reflects the cash flow and reality of the business
- Provides legal protections for both sides
- Leaves room for change if life happens

This chapter showed you just how flexible the options are—because flexibility is the key to making internal transitions possible.

Don't be afraid to get creative. Don't assume you need to follow a rigid script. As long as the numbers work and the risks are addressed, you can build a deal that works for you.

And if you're the seller? Remember that you're not just handing over a business. You're handing someone an opportunity they couldn't otherwise access. That has value. And you deserve to be paid well—for the business itself, and for the role you play in making the transition possible.

Structure is power. And when done right, it becomes the bridge between dreams and done deals.

6

STRUCTURING
THE DEAL

SECTION 1: DEAL STRUCTURES 101

When most small business owners think about selling their company, they imagine a clean break: one big check, one final signature, and a retirement party. But internal succession doesn't work like that. These deals are slower, messier, and more personal—but they're also often *more profitable* and *more sustainable* in the long run.

Internal succession deals can take many forms, but they all share one thing in common: they're built on **trust, time, and customization.** Unlike selling to a third-party buyer, you're not working with a stranger who's putting down 100% cash. You're working with someone inside the company—an employee, manager, or family member—who is likely financing the deal over time, often using the profits of the business itself.

Below are the most common internal deal structures used in small business transitions, with real-world examples of how they've worked.

1. Straight Sale with Seller Financing

In this model, the business is sold outright, but instead of the buyer securing outside funding, the seller acts as the bank. The buyer makes a down payment, then repays the rest over time—typically 5 to 10 years—using business profits.

Pros:
- Clean, simple structure
- Seller retains income stream over the payout period
- Buyer doesn't need to secure a bank loan

Cons:
- High risk for seller if the buyer fails
- Seller often remains emotionally invested until fully paid

Example: When Jeff retired from his auto repair business, he sold it to his long-time shop manager, Marcus. Marcus paid 10% of the $400,000 purchase price up front, and Jeff financed the remaining $360,000 over 7 years at 5% interest. Marcus pays $5,088/month and now runs the business independently, while Jeff receives consistent monthly income through the loan.

2. Gradual Buy-In

This is one of the most common internal succession paths. The successor purchases a small share of ownership (e.g. 5–10%) to start, then increases their stake gradually over time. Payments may come from their salary, a profit-share agreement, or personal savings.

Pros:
- Low upfront risk for both parties
- Builds loyalty and leadership gradually
- Allows for long-term mentorship and smoother cultural transition

Cons:
- Can take 10+ years to fully transition ownership
- Requires formal agreements at each phase
- If the relationship sours mid-way, disentangling can be tricky

Example: Sarah started as an assistant at a boutique dog grooming business. Over 12 years, she bought into the company in 5% chunks, funded through her year-end bonuses and a profit-sharing arrangement. When the founder retired, Sarah owned 60% of the business and bought the remaining 40% through a seller-financed agreement. The transition was seamless, and not a single client left.

3. Profit Share with Performance Milestones

Instead of buying in with cash, the successor earns equity by hitting performance goals: growing revenue, improving margins, or reaching strategic targets. Once milestones are achieved, they receive ownership shares as part of their compensation.

Pros:
- Motivates performance and accountability
- No cash needed upfront
- Aligns successor's goals with company growth

Cons:
- Requires clearly defined targets and tracking systems
- The IRS may view earned equity as compensation (taxable)
- Can feel subjective or cause conflict if expectations shift

Example: Rafael was the operations manager at a specialty bakery. The founder wasn't ready to sell the business outright but knew she needed to reduce her involvement. They designed a performance-based path to ownership:
- Rafael earned **10% equity** by increasing catering revenue by 30% over 18 months.
- He earned **another 10%** by improving the bakery's gross margins by 5%.
- When he successfully launched a profitable line of wholesale products, he earned **15% more**.

- His final milestone—opening and managing a second location while maintaining profitability—earned him an additional **15%**.

At this point, Rafael owned **50% of the business**, and profits had grown significantly. The founder, now semi-retired, began **taking her earnings through real-time profit distributions** rather than selling more equity. Rafael, now the full-time operator, continued earning equity through business development benchmarks until he eventually reached 100% ownership—without either party ever taking on debt or risking large upfront investments.

4. Hybrid Models

Many real-life deals are a combination of the above. A successor may start with a small cash buy-in, earn additional equity through performance, and complete the purchase with a seller-financed buyout. The beauty of internal succession is that it's *flexible*—as long as both sides are aligned on the goal.

What matters most is clarity: both parties should understand the timeline, terms, responsibilities, and what happens if the plan goes off-track. The structure you choose should fit your business's cash flow, your successor's financial capacity, and your mutual risk tolerance.

Example: Julie ran a successful event planning firm and brought on her junior partner, Denise, through a hybrid succession model. Denise paid $25,000 upfront for a 10% stake, earned another 10% through performance, and financed 30% through monthly payments. After two years of successfully managing operations, she completed a second seller-financed deal to purchase the remaining 50%. The flexible structure gave Julie peace of mind and gave Denise time to grow into full ownership while preserving the culture and client relationships they'd built together.

SECTION 2: TIMELINES AND TRANSITION PERIODS

If there's one thing internal succession isn't, it's fast.

Unlike selling your business to a third party, which often culminates in a 60-to-90-day sprint to closing, internal transitions take place **over years—not months.** And that's by design. The extended timeline gives both parties a chance to adapt, grow, and de-risk the transition. It also protects the business, the staff, and the customer base from a sudden jolt in leadership.

The most successful internal successions typically unfold over **5 to 20 years.** That may sound like a long time—especially if you're feeling ready to retire—but the truth is, that timeline reflects what's already happening under the surface. If you've been grooming someone to take over, they've probably been running large parts of the business already. This section is about making that transition **official, intentional, and stable.**

Why These Deals Take So Long

The core reason? The **buyer is growing into the role** and often using the business itself to finance the purchase. If the buyer had hundreds of thousands of dollars in cash, the timeline would be shorter—but in most internal transitions, the buyer pays over time, and ownership changes gradually.

Beyond financing, a longer timeline also:
- Allows the seller to **step back in stages** instead of vanishing overnight
- Lets clients, staff, and vendors adjust to new leadership slowly
- Builds trust in the successor's ability to manage the business independently
- Gives the buyer time to build confidence, financial skills, and leadership presence

A fast transition is tempting, but it's rarely sustainable. The goal isn't just to sell the business—it's to **pass it on without breaking it.**

Phased Transitions: How It's Done

There's no single formula, but most phased transitions follow a pattern like this:

Year 1–2: Ownership Begins, but Control Remains

- The buyer starts with partial ownership or a profit-share role
- The seller retains operational control and acts as mentor
- Payments begin (or performance milestones are established)
- The seller begins pulling back from day-to-day management

Year 3–5: Shared Leadership

- The buyer manages operations, finances, and staff
- The seller stays involved at a strategic level (oversight, high-level decisions)
- Ownership increases, either through vesting or buy-in
- The seller may move off-site or reduce hours significantly

Year 6+: Full Ownership and Independence

- The buyer becomes the face of the business
- Seller exits completely or stays on as an informal advisor or consultant
- Final payments or equity transfers are completed
- The new owner takes full control of banking, legal, marketing, and key decisions

This timeline can compress or stretch depending on the business, the successor's experience, and the financial arrangement. But the principle is the same: **transfer leadership before transferring the title.**

Common Mistakes in Timing

1. Stepping Back Too Soon

Some sellers want out so badly they vanish the moment a deal is signed. This can create chaos—especially if customers and staff see the successor as "junior" or "temporary." Without a clear, visible handoff, the business can lose trust and stability.

2. Hanging On Too Long

On the flip side, some sellers stay too involved and unintentionally undermine the successor. They don't let go of the reins, contradict decisions, or continue acting like the boss—eroding the buyer's authority and confidence.

3. Delaying Operational Handover

Some owners wait to transfer operational duties until the final year of the deal. By then, the buyer may not be prepared—or may have grown resentful. Successful transitions give the buyer *real responsibility* early in the process.

Planning for Your Transition Timeline

Every business is different, but here are some key questions to guide your timeline:
- When do you want to stop working full-time?
- When do you want to stop managing staff?
- When do you want to stop handling financials?
- When do you want to be fully out of the business?
- What does "out" actually mean to you? (Retired? Advisory? Available for questions?)

Work backward from your ideal "exit" date, then map out a series of **milestones:**

- Year X: Successor takes over scheduling
- Year Y: Successor runs payroll and budgeting
- Year Z: Seller moves to part-time or off-site

Document these milestones in your succession agreement—not just to protect yourself, but to set clear expectations for the buyer.

SECTION 3: OWNERSHIP VS. CONTROL

In an internal succession, **ownership and control are not the same thing**—and they don't have to transfer at the same time. In fact, it's often better when they don't.

Many founders assume that once they sell part of the business, they need to give up control. Others believe they can't let go of control until the very last payment is made. But internal succession allows for something far more nuanced: **staggered transitions,** where decision-making power and equity are separated, transferred at different speeds, and structured to fit the real needs of the business— not just the legal paperwork.

This section explores how to **decouple ownership from authority,** how to balance risk and autonomy, and how to create an orderly path from founder-led to successor-led without creating chaos.

Why Separate Ownership and Control?

The successor might need to run the business before they can afford to own it.

The seller might want to retain oversight even after giving up majority ownership.

This is common, especially in deals where:
- The buyer is new to leadership or managing finances
- The seller is staying involved for several years
- The business has large contracts, key clients, or high liability exposure

In these cases, the parties may agree to **gradually shift both ownership and operational control**—but on different timelines. Done right, this gives the buyer time to grow into the role while still protecting the business from premature or unstable leadership.

Control Can Be Shared

"Control" doesn't have to be all-or-nothing. It can be shared, segmented, or phased in over time.

You might transfer:
- **Day-to-day management** (first)
- **Hiring and HR responsibilities** (later)
- **Financial authority** (after that)
- **Strategic decision-making and long-term planning** (last)

At each stage, you can define:
- What decisions the successor can make solo
- What requires joint sign-off
- What the seller retains authority over until a trigger is met (e.g., payment, performance, time)

Voting Rights vs. Equity

In a gradual buy-in, it's common for the successor to have **minority ownership without voting control**—at least early on.

Example: Sarah owns 20% of the business but doesn't have decision-making authority until she reaches 40%. The operating agreement specifies that until that milestone is hit, all strategic decisions require majority shareholder (i.e., seller) approval.

This structure protects the seller while letting the buyer build ownership over time.

It also prevents problems like:
- A successor making major changes too early
- Disagreements about strategy or spending

- External stakeholders (like vendors or lenders) getting mixed messages

A simple **two-tiered structure** works well:
1. **Economic rights** (e.g., profit-sharing, equity vesting)
2. **Governance rights** (e.g., voting, signing contracts, making strategic hires)

You don't have to give both at once.

Assigning Authority in Writing

Don't assume this will "work itself out." It won't. Define control clearly in your legal agreements—especially if:
- Ownership is transferring before full payment
- The business is client-facing or compliance-heavy
- You're concerned about protecting brand, staff, or culture

A good lawyer can write clauses that:
- Grant limited decision-making rights to the buyer
- Require co-signatures or co-approval for big decisions
- Pause the transfer of control if benchmarks aren't hit
- Allow the seller to step back in temporarily if necessary

This isn't about distrust—it's about protecting both parties and the business itself.

Think in Phases, Not Percentages

Instead of thinking in percentages of ownership ("I'll give 10% per year"), think in **phases of responsibility:**

Example Phasing Plan:
- **Phase 1: Assistant Manager** → Learns back-end systems, HR, customer retention
- **Phase 2: General Manager** → Runs operations, leads staff meetings, signs off on budgets
- **Phase 3: Partner** → Oversees hiring, payroll, and contracts; begins attending strategy meetings
- **Phase 4: Managing Partner** → Makes all operational decisions; begins equity buyout

- **Phase 5: Owner** $\rightarrow$ Full legal and financial responsibility

This model helps both sides track progress, avoid confusion, and build confidence step by step.

What to Watch Out For

1. Too Much Authority Too Soon

Giving the buyer control before they're ready—or before equity has transferred—can backfire. Staff may resist the shift. The seller may feel sidelined. Clients may lose confidence.

Mitigation: Start with limited control and increase it through a written plan tied to performance.

2. Too Little Authority for Too Long

If the successor is doing all the work but has no authority to make real decisions, resentment builds—and they may walk away before the deal is done.

Mitigation: Give meaningful control early in the process, even if it's limited in scope.

3. No Clear Path

If there's no plan for how control will shift, decisions get bottlenecked. Staff is confused. The successor never fully "steps into" the role.

Mitigation: Create a phased plan with timelines, decision rights, and triggers for each level of control.

Bottom Line

In an internal succession, **you don't have to give it all up at once.** Ownership can move faster or slower than operational control—and vice versa. The best transitions are customized, staged, and grounded in clear expectations.

If you're the seller: you can keep control longer while letting go of ownership, or you can let the successor run the business while retaining final decision rights until payment is complete.

If you're the buyer: understand that earning trust often comes before full authority. Show up like an owner before you become one—both in responsibility and in mindset.

Define everything. Put it in writing. Then walk the path, one phase at a time.

SECTION 4: WHAT HAPPENS IF IT FALLS APART

No one enters a succession deal expecting it to fail—but some do. Life changes. Expectations shift. People grow in different directions. And sometimes, even with the best intentions, the deal just doesn't work out.

That doesn't mean internal succession was a bad idea. It just means the deal structure didn't account for what happens **when things go wrong.**

This section covers the safety mechanisms every succession deal needs: how to press pause, back out, or take back control—without burning down the relationship or the business.

Why Internal Deals Sometimes Fall Apart

Internal transitions are often more personal than external sales—and that's both a strength and a risk. When deals collapse, it's usually for one of these reasons:

- **Buyer burnout**—they realize they don't want to run the business after all
- **Performance issues**—the business underperforms, payments fall behind

- **Misaligned expectations**—one party wants to go faster (or slower) than the other
- **Life changes**—illness, divorce, a move, or a family emergency
- **Unclear boundaries**—the seller and buyer keep stepping on each other's toes

The good news? Most of these issues can be managed **if the right structures are in place from the beginning.**

The Importance of Exit Ramps

Every internal succession plan should include **a way out**—not because you expect to use it, but because having it makes the whole process more secure.

A strong deal gives both parties clarity on:
- What happens if the buyer stops paying
- What happens if the seller wants to sell to someone else
- What happens if the relationship breaks down
- What happens if the business performance tanks

These "what ifs" don't need to be scary. They just need to be acknowledged, agreed upon, and written into the deal.

Key Protections to Include

1. Clawback Clauses

These allow the seller to **reclaim a portion (or all) of the transferred equity** under specific conditions—usually tied to payment default, failure to meet performance benchmarks, or breach of contract.

Importantly, this is not a buyback. The equity is **reverted** to the seller automatically, without refund or compensation to the buyer. It must be clearly defined in the operating or purchase agreement and written by a qualified attorney.

Example clause: *"If the buyer is more than 90 days delinquent on any required payments, the seller shall have the right to reclaim* *up to 50% of any equity transferred to date, effective immediately. The reclaimed equity shall revert to the seller without refund or compensation to the buyer."*

What Happens After a Clawback?

Scenario:
- Buyer earns 30% over 3 years
- Buyer becomes 90+ days delinquent
- Clawback clause is triggered → 15% equity reverts
- Buyer now owns 15%, seller owns 85%

If the buyer recovers: The deal continues, possibly with extended terms or paused vesting.

If the buyer cannot recover: The deal may terminate or trigger a buyback clause.

2. Step-In Rights

These give the seller the right to **temporarily resume control** of the business if it's underperforming or at risk.

Example: When Sasha fell behind on payroll taxes while running the family's third-generation hardware store, her father—who had financed the deal—invoked a step-in clause. He resumed oversight for six months, helping restructure vendor debt and improve cash flow. Sasha returned to full control once the business stabilized.

3. Pause Clauses

Pause clauses let either party temporarily **suspend payments or decision-making shifts** without triggering default.

Example: Jordan, a co-owner in a landscaping company succession plan, was diagnosed with cancer and underwent surgery. The agreement included a pause clause: payments and equity vesting were paused for 4 months during treatment. The deal resumed once he returned to work, with the term extended by 4 months to keep the structure intact.

4. Trial Periods

Trial periods provide a **test phase** for leadership before equity or full control is transferred.

Example: Priya had managed a tutoring center for six years and was preparing to take over. Her agreement required a 12-month trial period in which she assumed full operations, met revenue benchmarks, and maintained staff retention. Only after completing the trial successfully did her first equity stake vest. The trial gave both sides confidence in her leadership.

5. Buyback Options

Buyback clauses protect the deal if one party decides to exit. They establish a fair, pre-agreed valuation formula and timeline.

Example: When Max, a graphic design firm successor, decided to move out of state to support his spouse's career, the agreement's buyback clause kicked in. The seller bought back Max's 40% equity using the original valuation formula (3x trailing 12-month SDE). The deal had a clause stating all buyback disputes would be settled by a neutral CPA, which prevented a messy fallout.

SECTION 5: OPERATING AGREEMENT NEEDS A BUY-SELL CLAUSE

A **Buy-Sell Agreement** (often baked into the operating agreement or deal contract) should cover this exact scenario.

Typical provisions include:

- **Right of First Refusal (ROFR):** The seller (or the company itself) gets the right to **buy back the equity** before it can be sold to anyone else.
- **Approved Buyer Clause:** The seller may restrict sales to third parties—especially **non-employees or competitors.**
- **Valuation Method:** Equity is priced using a **pre-agreed formula** (e.g., 3x SDE or appraised value)—not whatever the departing owner feels it's worth.

Example Clause: *"If the Buyer seeks to transfer any portion of their equity to a third party, the Seller shall have the right of first refusal. The equity shall be valued at three times the trailing twelve months of SDE. If the Seller declines to purchase, the Buyer may solicit other offers, subject to approval by the Seller or a designated majority of ownership."*

What Happens in Practice?

Option A: Seller Buys It Back

Kate, the original owner, can repurchase the 50% at the agreed valuation. This restores her to 100% ownership and gives her the option to:
- Restart the succession process with someone else
- Sell the business outright
- Continue operating solo

Option B: New Internal Buyer Steps In

Kate may invite another staff member (e.g., the assistant manager) to buy in using a revised succession deal, starting with the 50% stake that became available.

Option C: No Sale Allowed to Outsiders

If the agreement doesn't allow outside buyers—or requires approval—the deal may **pause until the parties renegotiate** or an internal successor is found.

What If There's No Clause?

If the agreement didn't account for this scenario, things can get ugly:
- Buyer may demand an unrealistic price
- Seller may have to buy back at a premium
- Buyer could sue for the right to liquidate their stake

Prevention is key. Always have a **Buy-Sell clause** and a valuation method written into the deal—*especially* as equity starts to vest.

Summary: If a Buyer with 50% Wants Out

- The **seller should have the first option to buy** the shares back.
- The **valuation should be predetermined,** not emotional or market-based.
- The **deal should block unauthorized sales** to outside parties.
- Ideally, there's a **clear process and timeline** to resolve the exit smoothly.

Real-World Near-Miss

Chloe had worked at a dog daycare for 9 years and began buying in under a performance-based plan. After 18 months of managing the business, she realized she didn't want to be a business owner—she wanted to work with animals, not worry about payroll and taxes.

Thankfully, the seller had included a trial equity clause: ownership would only vest after 24 months of operational leadership. Chloe stepped down, and the seller resumed full control without a legal fight or hard feelings.

How to Talk About Failure—Before It Happens

One of the most important parts of internal succession planning is **normalizing the idea that the deal might need to change.** That doesn't mean it's doomed. It means you're planning like professionals.

Some language to consider using in your agreements:

"If either party feels the arrangement is no longer viable, we agree to meet with a neutral third-party advisor within 30 days."

"This agreement may be revisited annually to adjust terms based on financial performance, buyer availability, or unforeseen events."

"All parties agree that unforeseen life changes are possible. This agreement provides for modification or termination under mutually agreed-upon conditions."

These clauses reduce tension and keep communication open— so if something does go wrong, you're not starting from zero.

Bottom Line

If you structure your deal like everything will go perfectly, you're setting yourself up for conflict.

If you structure your deal like **real life will happen**—with clear boundaries, contingency plans, and exit ramps—then even the hardest moments won't break the relationship or the business.

Hope for the best. Plan for the rest.

SECTION 6: COMPOSITE CASE STUDY—FROM EMPLOYEE TO OWNER IN 10 YEARS

Business Name: Morning Bell Coffee Roasters
Location: Portland, Oregon
Industry: Specialty coffee roasting and retail
Employees: 12
Annual SDE: $175,000

Agreed Valuation: $525,000 (3x SDE)
Seller: Kate, 58, founder and owner for 22 years
Buyer: Luis, 34, general manager with 8 years of experience in the company

The Structure

Kate wanted to retire slowly while ensuring the business she built remained in capable hands. Luis had managed day-to-day operations for the past 3 years and expressed interest in buying the business—but had no personal savings, no home equity, and a moderate credit score. No bank would lend to him.

They structured a **10-year internal succession** based on performance and profit:

- No down payment
- 10-year seller-financed deal at 6% interest
- Monthly payments of $5,828.58
- Ownership vests in phases based on performance + payment milestones

The Timeline

They agreed to a gradual transfer of both equity and control:

Years 1–2:
- Luis managed daily operations
- Kate retained full legal ownership and final decision-making power
- Luis began making payments and earned **10% equity** each year

Years 3–5:
- Luis received **additional control:** hiring authority, supplier negotiations, and budget approval
- Equity continued vesting at 10% per year, reaching **50% ownership by end of year 5**
- Kate moved to a part-time role and focused on mentoring Luis

Years 6–10:
- Luis became managing partner
- All decisions required his sign-off, with Kate in an advisory-only role
- Ownership continued vesting until Luis reached **100% equity at the end of year 10**

Financing and Profit Strategy

Payments came entirely from business profits. To support this:
- Luis expanded online sales
- Introduced a wholesale subscription model for local offices
- Raised prices slightly, which the loyal customer base accepted

These changes increased net income, allowing Luis to pay on time and reinvest in growth.

Legal Protections

The agreement included several smart guardrails:

Clawback Clause

If Luis missed more than two payments in a rolling 12-month period, Kate could reclaim up to 50% of vested equity. Fortunately, this clause was never triggered.

Step-In Rights

In year 3, when equipment delays disrupted wholesale orders, Kate exercised her temporary step-in clause to assist with vendor renegotiations.

Pause Clause

In year 6, Luis took a two-month medical leave after an accident. A pause clause allowed payments and equity transfer to freeze without default, extending the deal by 60 days.

Trial Period

The first 12 months were structured as a leadership trial. If Luis hadn't met key metrics—profit growth, client retention, staff satisfaction—the deal could have been terminated without penalty.

Buyback Option

If either party chose to exit, equity would be valued at 3x trailing 12-month SDE, with Kate given first right of refusal.

Outcome

Luis completed the deal in **year 9**, one year ahead of schedule. Kate transitioned fully into retirement with peace of mind—and a reliable income stream of $5,828.58 per month during the buyout.

Luis retained all staff, expanded to a second location, and began mentoring the assistant manager with plans to one day offer her a similar opportunity.

Lessons from the Morning Bell Case
1. **No cash doesn't mean no deal.** With a solid business and mutual trust, seller financing and performance-based equity made ownership possible.
2. **Structure trumps speed.** A long timeline gave everyone space to grow, adapt, and protect what mattered.
3. **Clarity equals confidence.** Written agreements covering worst-case scenarios created safety, stability, and long-term alignment.

SECTION 7: WHEN THE BUYER WANTS OUT MID-DEAL

Not every exit is triggered by failure. Sometimes the buyer—despite making progress, earning equity, and doing everything right—decides they no longer want to own the business.

Maybe they got a job offer in another state. Maybe a family situation changed. Maybe they simply realized: this isn't their dream after all.

This scenario becomes especially complicated when the buyer **already owns a significant equity stake,** like 30%, 40%, or even 50%. If you haven't planned for this, it can bring the entire deal—and business—into chaos.

What Should Happen (If You Planned Ahead)

This is where a **Buy-Sell Agreement** or strong exit language in your operating agreement becomes critical. It should define:

- **Who has the right to buy the departing owner's shares first** (usually the seller or the company itself)
- **Whether the buyer can sell their equity to an outsider** (often prohibited without approval)
- **How the departing owner's shares will be valued** (e.g., 2.5–3x trailing 12-month SDE)

Realistic Options

Option A: Seller Buys It Back

The seller regains full ownership. The buyer exits cleanly. The business continues or finds a new successor.

Option B: New Internal Buyer Steps In

Another employee—perhaps already being groomed— purchases the available equity and continues the succession plan.

Option C: Forced Hold / No Sale Allowed

If the agreement restricts outside sales, the buyer may have to hold the equity until the company buys it back or a new internal successor is found.

Sample Clause

"If the buyer wishes to exit prior to completion of the agreement, the seller and/or company shall have the right of first refusal to

repurchase the buyer's equity at a valuation equal to three times trailing 12-month SDE. No equity may be sold or transferred to a third party without written approval from the seller."

What If There's No Clause?

Without this protection:

- The buyer may demand a payout the business can't afford
- They could seek an outside buyer—possibly a competitor
- The seller could be forced to repurchase shares at a high cost—or lose control

The result? A legal and financial mess.

The Fix: Plan Early

As soon as equity begins to vest—even a small percentage—**build in an exit plan.** This isn't pessimism. It's professionalism.

Put it in writing:

- Valuation method
- Who gets first dibs
- Who must approve sales
- What timeline is allowed for payout or replacement

Bottom Line: Internal succession means thinking like co-owners— because that's what you are. Make sure both sides know how to exit with dignity, fairness, and a clean path forward.

SECTION 8: SUMMARY AND TAKEAWAYS

Internal succession isn't a transaction—it's a process. And that process needs to be built on more than just goodwill and a handshake. It needs to be structured.

Structure is what turns a vague promise ("I'll sell you the business someday") into a working plan. It's what protects both parties if things go wrong. It's what keeps the business running smoothly while ownership and control change hands.

The best internal succession deals are:
- **Flexible** enough to accommodate real life
- **Clear** enough to prevent confusion
- **Strong** enough to survive setbacks
- And **fair** enough to keep both parties motivated

Here's what we covered in this chapter:

Key Takeaways

1. There's no one right structure—but there must be structure.
Straight sales, gradual buy-ins, performance-based equity, seller financing, SBA hybrids—there's a model for every situation. Your job is to find the one that fits your business and your people.

2. Ownership and control don't have to transfer together.
They can—and often should—be separated and phased in over time. Think in milestones, not moments.

3. The timeline is longer than most people think.
Internal deals often take 5 to 20 years to complete. That's not a bug—it's a feature. Slow transitions build trust and stability.

4. Protect the downside.
Clawbacks, step-in rights, trial periods, and buyback clauses aren't signs of mistrust—they're signs of professionalism.

5. Plan for the worst so you can focus on the best.
When exit ramps are built in, you can move forward with confidence—even when life throws surprises.

6. Structure turns successors into owners.

It's not just about financing—it's about responsibility, mentorship, legal clarity, and emotional readiness.

If You're the Seller...

- Don't rush the exit.
- Be honest about what kind of control you want to keep (and for how long).
- Use the deal structure to get paid fairly **and** protect your legacy.
- Give your successor room to grow—but build in guardrails for when things wobble.

If You're the Successor...

- You don't need a giant check—you need a plan, and a partner.
- Show up like an owner before you become one.
- Ask for clarity, not control.
- Earn trust through performance, not promises.

Internal succession works best when it's built intentionally—with eyes wide open, a strong structure beneath it, and a shared belief that this business is worth handing down, not just selling off.

Up next: We'll explore how to **prepare the business itself** for a successful transition—from financial clean-up to systems documentation to culture-building. Because no matter how well-structured your deal is, the business itself has to be ready to survive without you.

7
LEGAL FRAMEWORKS THAT PROTECT YOU

When you enter into an internal succession deal, you're not just handing off a business—you're putting your financial future and personal legacy into someone else's hands. It's a high-stakes move that demands thoughtful legal preparation. Too many small business owners rely on trust, verbal agreements, or handshake deals. And while trust is important, it is not a strategy. It's certainly not enforceable in court.

The goal of this chapter is to walk you through the legal frameworks that protect your income stream, intellectual property, brand, and ability to walk away cleanly if the deal falls apart. We'll cover the core documents you need, the clauses that make or break a good contract, and how to find an attorney who understands the nuances of internal sales. Done right, your legal setup will serve as your guardrails, allowing you to transition out confidently without constantly looking over your shoulder.

Why Legal Protection Matters

An internal sale is emotionally different from a third-party sale. You're not selling to a stranger with a briefcase full of cash. You're selling to someone you know—a long-time employee, a trusted manager, or even a family member. That relationship can feel personal, familial, or collaborative. And that's where the danger lies.

Many owners skip or downplay the legal process in the name of trust. After all, "she would never screw me over" or "he knows the business like the back of his hand." But when pressure hits—when the business hits a rough quarter, or your successor starts to burn out, or their spouse starts asking tough questions about cash flow—those personal bonds are no substitute for a legally binding agreement.

Case Example: Family Fallout

Consider Bob, who owned a successful HVAC company in Ohio. He began transitioning the business to his son-in-law, Eric, without any formal agreement. For two years, Eric ran the day-to-day operations and paid Bob "as they went." When a recession hit, Eric cut payments to conserve cash, claiming he needed to pay staff first. Bob had no promissory note, no purchase agreement, and no clause to reclaim control. Their relationship deteriorated quickly, and Bob was left without income or legal standing.

Think of legal protections as your parachute. You hope you never have to pull it, but if you find yourself in freefall, you'll be glad it's there. Legal frameworks don't just protect you from disaster—they reduce misunderstandings, clarify expectations, and provide a roadmap when things get complicated, which they inevitably will.

The Core Legal Documents You Need

Every internal succession deal should be backed by a suite of legal documents that reflect your specific structure, goals, and timeline. These documents vary slightly depending on whether you're selling stock, transitioning shares in an S Corp, or changing LLC ownership percentages, but the fundamentals are the same.

Purchase Agreement

This is the heart of your deal. It spells out the agreed-upon price for the business, the timeline for payment, how ownership will be transferred, and under what conditions the deal can be terminated or modified. It includes terms for installment payments, consequences for missed payments, and your rights as the seller during the transition.

Example: The Builder Clause

Janet sold her boutique architecture firm to her lead designer over five years. The purchase agreement included a clause that required the buyer to maintain at least two ongoing commercial contracts per quarter. If this benchmark wasn't met, payments paused until business recovered. That single clause saved the deal when two major clients temporarily froze spending.

Promissory Note

If the buyer is paying you over time (which is the case in most internal sales), a promissory note outlines the repayment schedule, interest rate (if any), late fees, and what happens in the event of default. It formalizes the loan component of your deal and gives you legal recourse if the successor stops paying.

Example: Interest Incentive

One owner, Tom, built in a 4% interest charge but agreed to waive interest if the buyer made all payments on time for the first two years. It motivated the successor to prioritize timely payments.

Amendment to Operating Agreement or Shareholder Agreement

In a corporation or LLC, you'll need to update the governing documents to reflect the new ownership structure. This might include voting rights, profit distributions, or roles in decision-making. It's essential that these internal documents match the terms of your succession plan to avoid contradictions.

Consulting or Employment Agreement (If You're Staying Involved)

Many owners stay on during the transition to consult, mentor, or even handle specific duties. If so, a consulting or employment agreement clarifies your role, salary, hours, responsibilities, and how long you'll remain involved. It should also define the limits of your authority so that the successor can fully step into leadership.

Example: Defined Exit Plan

Raj stayed on as a consultant for 18 months after selling his medical billing firm. The agreement gave him 15 hours per month and explicitly stated he could not override management decisions. It prevented confusion and built the buyer's confidence.

Non-Compete / Non-Solicitation Agreement

Even if you have no intention of starting a competing business, your successor may feel nervous about your future moves. A non-compete agreement (reasonable in scope and geography) and a non-solicitation clause (preventing you from poaching employees or clients) offer mutual peace of mind.

IP and Brand Licensing Agreement

If the business name, logo, training methods, or other intellectual property belongs to you personally (rather than the business), you may choose to license those assets during the transition. This can allow you to retain long-term control or monetize your brand beyond the sale.

Example: The Name Lives On

Angela owned a wedding planning company with her personal name on the brand. She licensed the name for five years while her successor built new brand equity. The contract included quality standards for using her name.

Key Clauses That Protect You

Beyond having the right documents, your contracts need the right language. The devil, as they say, is in the details. Here are the most critical clauses to consider including:

Clawback Clause

A clawback clause gives you the right to regain some or all control of the business **if certain agreed-upon conditions are not met.** This is not always a total reversion of ownership—in fact, clawbacks can range from a full takeover to a temporary intervention.

Two Primary Types:
1. **Full Reversion Clawback:** You get the company back entirely, retaining all payments made so far.
2. **Temporary Intervention Clawback:** You step back in temporarily to stabilize operations, then the deal resumes.

Triggers might include:
- Revenue drops more than 20% for two consecutive quarters
- Two or more missed payments

- Ethical violations or breach of core terms
- Failure to meet client retention or service benchmarks

Example: Restaurant Recovery

When David sold his restaurant, the contract included a clawback clause if net margins dropped below 8% for more than three months. When the buyer slashed quality to cut costs, revenues plummeted. David was able to step in, stabilize operations, and later resell the business to someone new.

Soft Clawback Example: Coaching Period

Maria sold a wellness clinic to her lead therapist. After performance dipped and payments fell behind, the clawback clause let Maria re-enter for 90 days with operational control. She stabilized the team, relaunched the marketing plan, and then stepped back out, resuming the deal. That clause saved the deal *and* the relationship.

Clawback clauses can be customized to:
- Cap duration of re-entry (e.g., 90 days)
- Allow seller to appoint interim management
- Delay payment timelines
- Suspend equity transfers until recovery

Done right, clawbacks function as **early-warning systems,** not just exit ramps. They protect your future income *and* keep the deal from falling apart.

Pause Clause

Sometimes life happens. A pause clause allows the buyer to suspend payments for a limited time in the event of a major emergency (serious illness, natural disaster, etc.), with the understanding that the term will be extended accordingly. It protects both parties without blowing up the deal.

Final Deadline Clause

Even with pauses or extensions, you want a hard stop date. A final deadline clause ensures that the deal must be completed—payment made in full and ownership transferred—by a maximum number of years (typically no more than 10). This prevents a slow, endless drip of payments and gives both sides a long-term target.

No Prepayment Penalty

If your successor has a good year and wants to pay off the deal faster, they should be able to do so without penalty. This clause allows them to gain full ownership earlier, and it gets you paid faster—a win-win.

Performance Metrics

These can be tied to payments, equity transfer stages, or bonuses. For example: once net profit exceeds $250,000 per year for two consecutive years, ownership increases from 60% to 80%. Metrics should be realistic, measurable, and agreed upon in writing.

Dispute Resolution

Specify how disputes will be resolved: mediation first, then arbitration, and only then litigation, for example. You can also define the jurisdiction (county/state) where legal disputes must be filed. This avoids drawn-out court battles and surprise venue choices.

Finding the Right Attorney

Not all lawyers are equipped to handle internal succession. A general business attorney may default to external sale frameworks or miss the human dynamics involved. Your attorney needs to understand that:

- You are not getting a lump-sum payout.
- You care deeply about the successor and your staff.
- The business may need to fund the payments.
- You plan to stay involved (at least temporarily).

Start by asking other small business owners who've done internal deals. You want someone who understands **installment sales, family or employee transitions, and owner-retained rights.** In your first consultation, ask:

- Have you handled internal succession deals before?
- Can you help draft milestone-based clawback or pause clauses?
- Do you understand small business taxation?
- How do you typically structure seller-financed agreements?

Also, make sure your attorney is willing to collaborate with your accountant. The tax and legal planning go hand-in-hand.

Example: The Wrong Lawyer

Samantha chose her brother-in-law as her attorney—he specialized in real estate but offered to help. He drafted a one-page agreement without a payment schedule or any protections. Six months in, her buyer stopped paying. It cost her $20,000 in court and legal fees to get partial control back. She now tells every business owner: hire someone who does this all the time.

Customizing Legal Protection to Fit Your Deal

There is no one-size-fits-all contract. A good legal framework reflects the spirit of your deal, not just its letter. If your successor is a family member, you may want softer default triggers. If it's a manager buying you out over time, your promissory note may include performance bonuses. If you're keeping the brand name for a new venture, the licensing agreement must be crystal clear.

Revisit your documents annually during the transition. Update them as the business evolves, the payments progress, and the successor steps more fully into ownership. Legal agreements aren't carved in stone—they should evolve as your relationship and reality do.

Wrapping Up

Legal protection isn't about mistrust—it's about clarity. A strong legal framework builds confidence for both the seller and the buyer. It gives you the ability to exit cleanly if necessary, and it gives your successor the stability to succeed. Don't leave this part of the process to chance. Hire the right help, write the right documents, and build the deal on a solid foundation.

Up next, we'll dive into the dollars and cents of internal succession: how to fund the deal, what financing options exist for successors, and how to ensure that your exit plan is actually affordable for everyone involved.

8

TRANSITION PHASES THAT WORK

SECTION 1: WHY THE TRANSITION PHASE MATTERS

Most small business owners assume the hardest part of succession is choosing the right person or structuring the financial terms. Those are *crucial* decisions — but they aren't the ones that quietly make or break the business after the papers are signed. What truly determines whether an internal succession succeeds is how well the actual **day-to-day control** is handed over.

This phase is the long middle of the story—after the deal has begun, but before the seller is out. And in many ways, it's the most delicate part. It's not about spreadsheets or signatures; it's about **trust, perception, and leadership.**

If the transition of control is rushed, chaotic, or unclear, the successor struggles to gain credibility — and staff, clients, and vendors will instinctively continue turning to the founder. The business appears rudderless, the successor feels undermined, and the founder stays stuck in a loop of being "just a little bit too involved." Morale slips. Turnover creeps in. Customers question what's going on. Confidence, once shaken, can take years to rebuild—or never recover.

A Real-World Example: Burke's Auto & Tire, Flagstaff, Arizona

Take **Burke's Auto & Tire**, a thriving 6-bay repair shop in **Flagstaff, Arizona**. Founded by **Don Burke** in 1997, the shop had built a strong local reputation for honesty and quality. By 2020, Don was nearing retirement and had quietly struck a deal to sell the business over five years to his lead technician, **Maria Santos**, who had been with the shop for over a decade.

The purchase agreement was solid: Maria would pay Don $100,000 per year for five years, with Don remaining on payroll at $24,000 per year during the transition. But there was no detailed plan for *when* Maria would start handling key responsibilities—managing payroll, ordering inventory, dealing with complaints, negotiating vendor contracts. For the first year, Don still handled most of the big decisions, while Maria technically "owned" part of the business. Staff were confused. Customers still asked for Don. Maria was reluctant to make changes because she didn't want to "step on Don's toes."

By year two, the situation became tense. A key employee quit, citing confusion over who was in charge. A longtime supplier nearly dropped them after a delayed payment that no one caught. Don, frustrated by the lack of leadership, began quietly second-guessing the deal. Maria, overwhelmed and unsure, considered walking away.

Eventually, with the help of a business coach, they implemented a monthly transition timeline—Maria would take over one major area of operations each month, and Don would step back incrementally. Within six months, things stabilized. But the damage to morale and vendor confidence took time to rebuild.

The lesson: **A clear plan for transitioning control isn't optional—it's essential.**

Why Everyone Is Watching the Handoff

In a small business, leadership isn't abstract—it's visible. Customers see who answers emails. Employees see who leads meetings. Vendors know who signs the checks. If the successor doesn't *feel* like the new boss, people will act accordingly.

Without a clear transition:
- Staff will keep going to the founder with every problem.
- Clients may doubt the successor's authority or competence.
- The founder may feel pulled back in, creating resentment or dependency.
- The successor may hesitate to make needed changes, afraid of pushback or failure.

This transition phase is not just an operational concern—it's a psychological and cultural one. A successful handoff builds **momentum, legitimacy, and clarity.** A failed one plants doubt that never quite goes away.

The Emotional Tightrope

What makes this phase so challenging is that it's *not purely logical.* Both the seller and the buyer are dealing with identity shifts.
- For the **founder,** stepping back can feel like letting go of a part of themselves. Their name, reputation, and relationships are tied up in the business. Watching someone else steer— especially if they do it differently—can be uncomfortable or even threatening.
- For the **successor,** stepping forward is intimidating. They may fear they'll mess it up. They may worry they don't have the same charisma, knowledge, or trust. And they often want to "honor" the founder by holding back—which only delays their authority from taking root.

One way to ease this emotional tension is to treat the transition as a **defined leadership development process,** not just a vague overlap. This means making explicit:

What roles will shift when

Create a **transition matrix** that outlines when each of the following responsibilities will be handed off to the successor. This removes ambiguity and sets expectations on both sides.

Here's a sample list of roles that should be clearly scheduled:
- Hiring and firing employees
- Supervising and reviewing staff
- Managing payroll and benefits administration
- Handling customer service escalations
- Setting pricing and service rates
- Ordering supplies and managing vendor relationships
- Creating staff schedules
- Overseeing marketing and advertising
- Approving budgets and managing cash flow
- Handling bookkeeping and accounting
- Signing checks or initiating payments
- Filing taxes or working with accountants
- Renewing licenses, permits, and insurance policies
- Conducting staff meetings and training sessions
- Responding to legal or regulatory inquiries

In most internal transitions, the successor may already be doing **some** of these things—but not all. It's crucial to avoid the trap of "shared responsibility," which often means no one is fully accountable.

Instead, assign clear handoff dates. For example:
- *Month 3:* Maria begins approving all supply orders.
- *Month 5:* Maria takes over payroll and signs her first round of checks.

- *Month 7:* Maria leads her first quarterly budget meeting and reviews YTD spending.
- *Month 9:* All staff supervision and reviews are handled solely by Maria.

This isn't just about tasks—it's about symbolism. Each handoff signals to staff, vendors, and Maria herself that she is *becoming the business's true leader.*

How decisions will be made

This can't be left to gut feelings or case-by-case reactions. You need a **decision protocol** that defines:
- What types of decisions the successor can make alone
- What decisions require consultation with the seller
- What decisions must be formally reviewed or approved jointly
- How disagreements will be handled (tie-breaker process)
- For example, you might agree that:
- Maria can make independent purchases under $5,000
- All hiring decisions are hers, but terminations must be discussed with Don for the first 6 months
- Any legal matters or loans must be reviewed jointly
- If they disagree on a financial decision, the CPA will mediate

Formalizing this avoids confusion and unnecessary tension. It also gives the successor boundaries within which to grow.

What support structures are in place

Support isn't just emotional—it's **operational and advisory.** Here are examples of structures that help the successor thrive:
- **Weekly one-on-one meetings** with the founder to review wins, challenges, and upcoming decisions
- Access to a **bookkeeper or fractional CFO** who can provide financial clarity during the transition
- A **succession accountability calendar** (like a shared spreadsheet or project management tool)

- Written **Standard Operating Procedures (SOPs)** for all major business functions
- A designated **third-party advisor or coach** (paid or volunteer) who can give the successor a neutral sounding board
- Temporary overlap of roles (e.g., co-signing checks for 90 days) to provide oversight without micromanagement

Support doesn't mean babysitting—it means **infrastructure** to ensure the transition stays on track.

How the founder and successor will communicate

No, this doesn't just mean "by phone or email." It means setting a clear **communication rhythm and format,** such as:

- A **standing weekly check-in meeting**, preferably face-to-face
- A shared **Google Doc or dashboard** for tracking transition milestones and to-dos
- An agreement about when to text (e.g., urgent issues) vs. when to email (e.g., updates or non-urgent needs)
- An end-of-month **debrief and reflection** to discuss progress, flag concerns, and make adjustments

Some founders assume they'll "just be around if needed," but that's vague and leaves the successor guessing. Others overstay and second-guess decisions. A planned rhythm reduces emotional tension and promotes confidence on both sides.

This phase of transition isn't just about transferring authority—it's about building it, reinforcing it, and **demonstrating it clearly to everyone watching.**

SECTION 2: SETTING THE TIMELINE

One of the most common mistakes in internal succession is assuming the handoff will happen "organically." It won't. Without a clear, written timeline for how and when control shifts, even the best successor will flounder, and the seller may never fully step back.

Succession is not an event—it's a **series of deliberate milestones** over time.

The earlier and more clearly you define the transition timeline, the smoother the process will be. Ideally, the timeline should begin **before** any ownership is transferred and should run for **12 to 36 months**, depending on the business's complexity.

Why a Timeline Is Critical

A timeline serves four major functions:

1. **It sets expectations.** Both parties know what is happening and when—reducing surprises and misunderstandings.
2. **It builds accountability.** A written timeline creates shared responsibility for hitting milestones.
3. **It gives staff and clients confidence.** When people see an organized plan, they're more likely to trust the process.
4. **It prevents emotional drift.** Without a clear path, fear and inertia can take over. The founder hesitates. The successor second-guesses. The transition stalls.

The absence of a timeline is how a 2-year handoff turns into a 6-year limbo.

Key Phases in a Succession Timeline

While every transition will differ, most internal successions follow a similar flow. Below is a sample structure you can tailor to your business.

Phase 1: Observation and Shadowing (Months 1–3)

- Successor shadows the seller in all key areas.
- Attends meetings, vendor calls, staff reviews.
- Begins taking notes on processes and identifying training needs.
- May lead small tasks under supervision.

Example: In Tulsa, Oklahoma, a plumbing company called **Cooper Mechanical** began its handoff with weekly "ride-alongs." Founder **Steve Cooper** had his successor, **Jason Yamada**, accompany him on all major client visits and vendor negotiations. Jason didn't speak at first—just listened. By the end of month three, he could recite key client histories better than Steve.

Phase 2: Partial Handoff (Months 4–9)
- Successor begins leading defined areas (e.g., scheduling, payroll).
- Communication to staff begins to shift—employees are directed to go to the successor first.
- Successor begins signing checks, approving purchases, and taking point in meetings.
- Seller remains available as a backup, but only intervenes when needed.

Phase 3: Operational Control (Months 10–18)
- Successor is running daily operations independently.
- Staff report to the successor, not the founder.
- Successor manages vendors, hires staff, and runs budgets.
- Founder may remain involved in strategy or big-picture decisions only.

Case in point: In **Manchester, New Hampshire**, a dental practice called **Smile Studio** shifted control over 15 months. Founder **Dr. Elise Fournier** handed off financial operations and hiring by month 9, and by month 12, her successor **Dr. Ronny Pak** was leading weekly staff meetings and resolving patient issues. Elise stayed on for quarterly strategy lunches but kept her hands out of the daily grind.

Phase 4: Strategic Leadership (Months 18–24)

- Successor makes long-term planning decisions.
- May launch new products or services.
- Engages with advisors, CPAs, and legal counsel directly.
- Founder steps back entirely or moves to an advisory role.

Optional Phase 5: Final Exit (Months 25–36)

- Seller transitions out completely.
- May retain a seat on a board (if formed), or move to passive income status.
- Successor takes over public-facing leadership—speaking at events, doing media, joining industry associations.

In **Santa Rosa, California**, retail business **Wild Fig Mercantile** completed its handoff over 30 months. Founder **Greta Lewis** stayed on as a figurehead until her final year, then quietly exited, leaving successor **Monica Chen** fully in charge. The smoothness of that exit earned Monica a feature in the local business journal—and customer loyalty actually increased.

How to Build Your Timeline

1. **Start with the end date.** When will the founder be fully out? Work backwards from there.
2. **List all major control areas.** Use the list from Section 1—HR, finance, operations, etc.
3. **Assign target months** for each handoff.
4. **Build in review checkpoints** every 3 months to reassess the pace.
5. **Put it in writing**—use a shared document that both parties can see, edit, and update.

A sample milestone chart might look like this:

Week	Milestone
1	Shadowing: Attend all meetings
3	Begin managing staff schedule
6	Take over payroll and vendor ordering
9	Run staff meeting independently
12	Handle all customer escalations
15	Approve and manage marketing spend
18	Lead budget planning
24	Final strategic control transfer
30	Full exit of founder

Be Ready to Adjust

No timeline survives first contact with real life. Illness, market changes, staff turnover, or even emotional readiness can affect progress. That's okay. The timeline isn't a contract—it's a compass. What matters is that both parties return to it regularly, update it transparently, and **treat it as the structure that keeps momentum alive.**

If you're the founder, remind yourself: **letting go is a discipline.** The more clearly you define the handoff, the less likely you are to get pulled back into the day-to-day. And if you're the successor, know this: **gaining control takes courage**—and having a timeline proves you're not alone in it.

SECTION 3: GRADUAL HANDOFF OF RESPONSIBILITIES

One of the biggest mistakes in internal succession is assuming the new owner will naturally "figure it out" once the deal is underway. But without a deliberate, **step-by-step handoff of specific responsibilities,** most successors will either freeze under pressure or overreach and make costly missteps. A gradual handoff helps the successor **build confidence** while preserving continuity and minimizing risk.

Think of it like a pilot program. Before turning over full control, the founder gives the successor a series of increasingly complex tasks—allowing them to lead while still being coached and supported.

Why Gradual Matters

This method works because it balances three critical needs:
- The business keeps running smoothly.
- The successor learns without being thrown into the deep end.
- The founder can assess readiness and course-correct without undermining trust.

More importantly, a gradual handoff gives **everyone watching**—staff, clients, vendors—time to adjust. Authority isn't something you declare; it's something you demonstrate. Gradual handoff gives the successor time to earn that authority in the eyes of others.

What to Hand Off—and When

There's no universal order for which responsibilities get handed off first. It depends on the business, the skills of the successor, and how involved the founder still is in the day-to-day. That said, here's a general progression that works well in most small businesses:

Stage 1: Internal Operations

Start with tasks that affect internal systems more than external stakeholders:
- Creating staff schedules
- Ordering supplies and managing vendor deliveries
- Managing payroll (possibly with a bookkeeper)
- Running weekly staff meetings
- Handling employee questions or shift issues

In **Columbia, Missouri**, the owner of **Home Harvest Landscaping**, **Rob Garrett**, began handing over his company to longtime foreman **Chloe Miller** by first letting her run the scheduling board. She learned how to match crew capacity with job estimates and seasonal forecasts—a skill that later made budgeting easier when she took over cost control. For 60 days, Rob reviewed every schedule before it went out. By the third month, he stopped checking.

Stage 2: Client-Facing Leadership

Once the successor has proven they can handle internal systems, it's time to step into a more visible role:
- Responding to client complaints or escalations
- Presenting proposals and estimates
- Making follow-up calls to lapsed clients
- Managing reviews and public feedback
- Networking in the community

Often, this is where credibility is won—or lost. The successor has to develop their own communication style while holding to the standards and tone of the business. The founder's job here is to stay **present but silent** unless something goes off course.

Stage 3: Financial and Strategic Oversight

These are often the last tasks to be handed off, as they carry the most long-term impact:
- Approving budgets
- Reviewing monthly financials
- Signing checks and initiating payments
- Setting pricing strategy
- Reviewing legal documents or major contracts
- Deciding on capital investments (equipment, leases, hiring)

This is also where founders often struggle to let go. These decisions feel personal, and mistakes here can be expensive. But holding on too long tells everyone—especially the successor—that they're not really trusted.

One of the clearest examples of a successful financial handoff happened in **Asheville, North Carolina**, at a custom cabinetry company called **Blue Ridge Built**. Founder **Liam Trevors** had been managing all vendor relationships and pricing since 2006. When his successor **Jasmine Ortega** came on board, they spent three months reviewing every quote, margin report, and invoice together. On the first day of Month 4, Jasmine began submitting vendor orders and adjusting prices herself. Liam told suppliers in a formal letter that Jasmine had full decision-making authority. That one email changed everything: phone calls went to her, not him. The torch had been passed.

How to Structure the Handoff

Use a **handoff worksheet** or spreadsheet to track:
- What task is being handed off
- When it will happen
- What support or training will be provided
- What success looks like (e.g., "no missed payrolls for 3 months" or "maintains 5-star client ratings")
- When the founder will fully step away from involvement in that task

You can organize this into weekly or monthly goals, depending on your timeline.

Example Entry:

Task	Handoff Date	Training Method	Owner's Exit Date	Success Criteria
Payroll	Month 3	Bookkeeper tutorial + 2 trial runs	Month 4	Payroll submitted on time 3 months in a row
Client Quotes	Month 6	Observe 3 calls + shadow on email responses	Month 7	90% client approval on quote clarity

Task	Handoff Date	Training Method	Owner's Exit Date	Success Criteria
Staff Reviews	Month 9	Attend 1-on-1s with owner, then lead own	Month 10	No employee turnover in next 3 months

This tool keeps everyone accountable, and it helps prevent what we call **"yo-yo authority"**—when a founder gives away a task, but pulls it back at the first sign of trouble. That destroys trust and paralyzes the successor.

What If the Successor Struggles?

It's normal for some tasks to be rocky at first. That's why a gradual handoff works—it gives room for feedback and improvement. If the successor struggles:

- Don't take the task back. Instead, review what support is missing.
- Ask if they understood the expectations.
- Revisit the training method: was it clear, hands-on, and sufficient?

Sometimes a small tweak—like a template for writing client emails or a checklist for vendor orders—can make a big difference. And if performance continues to be an issue, it's better to find out during the handoff than a year after the founder walks away.

A gradual handoff is about building **trust, competence, and authority—in that order.** When done right, it creates a clean runway for the successor to take off, and for the founder to step back with confidence, knowing the business is in capable hands.

SECTION 4: LETTING GO WITHOUT VANISHING

Letting go is the hardest part of any internal succession. For many founders, the business is more than a livelihood—it's an identity, a legacy, and a reflection of decades of effort. Walking away entirely can feel like abandoning a child or erasing a part of yourself. But staying too involved can quietly undermine the very succession you worked so hard to build.

The solution is not to vanish—but to **exit with intention.** The goal is to reduce your operational presence while **remaining available in a structured, non-intrusive role.**

The Emotional Tightrope

Founders often oscillate between two extremes:

- **Micromanagement:** hovering over every decision, correcting the successor in front of staff, or stepping back in every time something goes wrong.
- **Abrupt withdrawal:** disappearing completely to "prove" they're letting go, leaving the successor unsupported and isolated.

Both approaches are damaging. The former erodes the successor's authority and confidence. The latter signals abandonment. The healthiest path is to **gradually withdraw** while remaining available as a mentor and backup.

In **Sarasota, Florida**, a boutique fitness studio called **Elevate Strength & Motion** struggled with this very issue. Founder **Jenna Blake**, after selling the business to her longtime manager **Tasha Reed**, tried to step away cold turkey. Within two months, Tasha was overwhelmed, staff morale dipped, and Jenna was fielding calls from confused clients. The solution? Weekly Friday coffee meetings where Tasha could review decisions, ask questions, and get Jenna's take. It wasn't micromanagement—it was mentorship. And it gave Tasha the confidence she needed to lead independently.

Redefining Your Presence Without Overshadowing

Founders don't need to disappear—they just need to **shift their role.**

Consider moving into one of the following identities:

- **Mentor:** available for regularly scheduled check-ins, but not involved in day-to-day decisions
- **Consultant:** offers specific advice on strategic issues (e.g., budgeting, expansion, major vendor changes)
- **Advisor/Board Member:** reviews quarterly goals, offers insights, but holds no operational authority
- **Brand Ambassador:** represents the business at select events but doesn't engage in internal matters

The key is to **be consistent.** If you're a mentor, don't randomly start fixing operational problems. If you're an advisor, don't quietly rewrite the staff schedule. Successors need to know where the lines are—and so does the rest of the team.

Tips for Letting Go Without Causing Chaos

1. **Set a final date for operational involvement.**
   Even if you'll still be mentoring, make it clear when you'll stop running the day-to-day. Put it in writing and stick to it.

2. **Create a structured communication rhythm.**
   For example: weekly meetings in the first 6 months, then monthly meetings for a year. This keeps input focused and prevents boundary creep.

3. **Resist rescuing.**
   Let the successor make mistakes—especially small ones. You can debrief later, but avoid stepping in mid-crisis unless absolutely necessary.

4. **Redirect others.**
   If staff or clients come to you with questions, train yourself to say: *"That's something [Successor's Name] is handling now—you'll want to go through them."* That single sentence builds authority faster than any title ever could.

5. Find something else to build.

One of the best ways to let go is to give your energy a new outlet — a nonprofit, a new business, a book, a sabbatical. Letting go is easier when you're moving toward something, not just away from something.

In **Boise, Idaho**, when **Marcus Fielding** exited his 14-year-old IT firm, **FieldTech Solutions**, he worried about irrelevance. He'd sold to his operations manager, **Theo Martinez**, and struggled not to jump in during tense client negotiations. His coach suggested starting a small side project: a tech literacy program for high schoolers. It gave Marcus a purpose—and Theo the space to lead.

What If You Can't Let Go?

Sometimes, despite best efforts, the founder simply can't step back. If that's you—or if you're working with someone in that position—it's time to ask why.

- Is it about fear of financial instability?
- Is it fear that the business won't be as good without you?
- Is it worry that your identity is too tied to your role?

None of those are shameful—but all of them are signs that the emotional transition hasn't caught up to the legal one. Consider involving a coach, therapist, or business advisor to unpack what's really holding you back.

Remember: **you're not just letting go of control—you're transferring legacy.** And legacy only lasts if you let others carry it.

SECTION 5: COMMUNICATING THE TRANSITION TO STAFF AND CLIENTS

A well-executed internal succession doesn't just depend on private agreements—it also depends on **public perception.** Staff and clients don't automatically recognize someone as the new leader just because paperwork was signed. They look for cues: Who's making decisions? Who's sending emails? Who's standing at the front of the meeting?

That's why a thoughtful **communication plan** is critical. You're not just changing leadership—you're managing a shift in loyalty, authority, and confidence.

Staff Need Clarity and Stability

When employees aren't sure who's in charge, morale drops, gossip spreads, and productivity suffers. Even worse, some may try to play both sides—asking the founder for one answer and the successor for another.

Avoid this dynamic by being **proactive and clear:**

1. **Make a formal announcement.**
   Host a staff meeting to introduce the transition. The founder should speak first, explain the "why" of the transition, and then formally endorse the successor. Then, the successor should speak—briefly but confidently—about their commitment to the team.

2. **Use strong, decisive language.**
   Phrases like:
   o *"Starting next month, [Successor Name] will be overseeing all operations."*
   o *"I've chosen [Successor] to lead this company forward, and I'm proud of that decision."*
   o *"Please direct all future questions or approvals to [Successor]."*

3. **Clarify roles and timelines.**
   Let the team know what changes immediately and what will shift over time. You don't have to explain the payment structure—just the chain of command.

4. Address concerns early.

Invite staff to submit questions or meet privately if they're unsure about anything. Transition-related anxiety is normal, especially for long-tenured employees. Silence breeds fear—transparency breeds loyalty.

At **Trail Ridge Veterinary Center** in **Boulder, Colorado**, founder **Dr. James Lin** was retiring after 22 years. His successor, **Dr. Megan Doyle**, was well-liked but relatively new. During the transition announcement, Dr. Lin stood beside her and said: *"You trusted me with your animals for two decades. I trust Megan the same way, and so should you."* That single statement calmed the room—and Megan's phone started ringing with support that same afternoon.

Clients and Vendors Need Reassurance

Clients and vendors want consistency. They don't like surprises—especially when it involves money, service, or relationships. If you've built a strong personal connection with them over the years, they'll need help understanding why this change is good for them.

Here's how to make that happen:

1. Send a letter or email from the founder.

Keep it short and sincere. The tone should be appreciative, optimistic, and confident in the successor's abilities.

"After 18 incredible years, I've begun the process of transitioning the business to [Successor's Full Name], someone I trust completely and who shares our commitment to excellence."

2. Introduce the successor by name.

Tell your clients a little about them—how long they've been with the company, their background, and why they're the right person to take the reins. Include a photo if appropriate.

3. **Keep key service touchpoints the same at first.**
   Don't change your logo, business hours, or billing practices right away. Let the relationship settle first—then modernize if needed.

4. **Offer a personal follow-up.**
   For VIP clients or long-term accounts, have the successor personally call or meet with them. Even 10 minutes of face time can go a long way in preserving trust.

5. **Update your website, email signatures, and social media.**
   Within the first 30 days, make sure the world knows the successor's name, title, and role. A lingering "contact the owner" button with the founder's face sends the wrong message.

Clear communication doesn't mean oversharing. You don't have to explain your payment structure, retirement timeline, or emotional journey. What matters is showing your community that this is a **thoughtful, stable transition—not a retreat or a reaction.**

Done right, communication creates what every succession needs most: **confidence.** And once confidence takes root, authority follows.

SECTION 6: REDEFINING THE OWNER'S ROLE

Once the successor begins running the day-to-day, the founder must answer a crucial question:

Who am I now?

In an internal succession, the founder doesn't disappear overnight—but they also don't get to keep being the boss. That in-between space requires a new identity, one that supports the successor without overshadowing them, and allows the founder to remain connected without becoming disruptive.

This isn't just a business decision—it's a personal one. Many founders underestimate how much their role at work has defined their sense of purpose, routine, and social connection. When the title fades, it can feel like something is missing.

Common Post-Transition Roles for Founders

Here are some clear, constructive roles a founder can shift into after the successor has taken control:

- **Mentor or Coach:** Offers advice and support, typically during scheduled meetings. Avoids unsolicited input.
- **Advisor or Board Member:** Participates in quarterly or strategic meetings. Reviews financials, plans, or major decisions.
- **Special Projects Lead:** Takes on legacy work, like documenting SOPs, launching a new product, or managing a one-time event.
- **Brand Ambassador:** Attends community or industry events. Promotes continuity and legacy without getting into operations.
- **Silent Owner:** Stays entirely out of day-to-day activity, collecting payments or dividends.

The key is to **choose one** and communicate it clearly. Mixing roles ("I'm just helping with one thing—oh, and also leading the staff meeting") leads to confusion and undermines the successor's authority.

The Emotional Adjustment

This stage often brings surprising emotions: sadness, resentment, anxiety, or even guilt for not feeling happier. That's normal. Founders who've been working 60-hour weeks for decades don't just "settle into free time." Some grieve the loss of urgency, visibility, or control.

In **Richmond, Virginia**, when **Carla Jennings** handed off her catering business, **Harvest Table Events**, to her protégé **Noah Patel**, she planned to stay involved "a little." But after three weeks of drifting, she realized she was lonely—and tempted to check every email. Instead, she set boundaries and started a new food blog, positioning herself as a storyteller, not an operator. It gave her a creative outlet and allowed Noah to fully step up.

Define It, Write It Down, Say It Aloud

Whatever role you choose, make it official:

- Write it into your succession agreement.
- Announce it to staff and vendors.
- Set a time period (e.g., "for the first 12 months") and revisit it at the end.

Redefining your role isn't the end of your story. It's the beginning of your next chapter—and the best ones come when you're no longer trying to hold the pen for someone else.

SECTION 7: HOW TO KNOW THE TRANSITION IS WORKING

By the time you're deep into the transition, the question becomes: **Is it working?** Not just on paper—but in practice.

Internal successions don't have clear breakpoints like external sales do. No ribbon-cutting. No champagne. It's a slow drift from one leadership identity to another. That's why it's important to step back periodically and assess whether the successor is **truly functioning as the leader**—and whether the business is responding to that leadership.

Signs the Transition Is Working

You don't need a business consultant to spot success. Here are practical, observable signs that the handoff is taking hold:

- **Staff now go to the successor first**—not the founder—when there's a problem.
- **The successor is making decisions independently** and communicating them confidently.
- **The founder is no longer looped into daily operations**—and things aren't falling apart.

- **Clients and vendors are addressing the successor by name** and treating them as the authority.
- **Key business metrics are stable or improving.** Revenue, staff retention, customer satisfaction—these don't have to skyrocket, but they shouldn't slide.
- **The successor is solving problems you never even hear about.** That's leadership.

One of the clearest indicators? The founder goes on vacation—or steps away for a week—and the business keeps humming.

That's exactly what happened at **Sunriver Outfitters**, a kayak and bike rental shop in **Bend, Oregon**. Founder **Tom Castellanos** had transitioned control to his niece, **Rachel Marin**, but still came in most days "just to check." It wasn't until Tom had jury duty for two weeks—and everything ran smoothly— that he finally said, *"I guess she really does have this."* From that point forward, Rachel took full control, and Tom stopped looking over her shoulder.

Red Flags That Need Attention

Even well-intentioned transitions can start to stall. Watch for these signs that the process may need a course correction:
- The successor is hesitant or constantly deferring to the founder.
- Staff still rely on the founder for approvals.
- Major decisions are being delayed out of fear or misalignment.
- Customers complain about confusion or inconsistent service.
- The founder is regularly pulled back into operations.

If these symptoms arise, don't panic—and don't rip up the plan.

Instead:
- Revisit the handoff timeline. Are certain responsibilities still unclear?
- Check in with the successor. Do they feel overwhelmed? Undersupported?

- Look at your own behavior. Are you creating dependency without realizing it?

Transitions don't have to be perfect—but they do have to move forward. If momentum has stalled, name it early, and **recalibrate with structure and grace.**

SECTION 8: SAMPLE TRANSITION TIMELINE (MINI CASE STUDY)

To make everything in this chapter more tangible, here's a real-world example of a structured internal succession transition—from first handoff to final exit. What follows is a simplified version of a 24-month timeline used successfully by a small business.

Case Study: Harbor & Pine Bookkeeping, Charleston, South Carolina

Founder: Alicia Mendoza

Successor: Simone Bradley

Business: Boutique bookkeeping firm with 9 clients and 4 part-time staff

Deal Structure: 5-year buyout, $80,000/year, with Alicia remaining on a $24,000 salary for Year 1 only

Goal: Full control to Simone in 24 months, while maintaining client retention and staff continuity

Transition Timeline Overview

Months 1–3: Shadowing + Introduction
- Simone observes all client meetings and internal processes.
- Joint announcement to clients: Alicia is beginning her transition, Simone is introduced by name.
- Alicia and Simone co-lead staff meetings.
- Simone begins drafting email communications and client reports for review.

Months 4–6: First Handoffs

- Simone takes full control of scheduling and internal staff coordination.
- Begins leading recurring client calls with Alicia present.
- First responsibility handoff: managing three of the nine client accounts directly.
- Alicia steps back from daily staff oversight.

Months 7–12: Operational Control

- Simone now handles payroll, invoicing, and AR tracking.
- Alicia reviews financials quarterly but no longer signs off on routine activity.
- Simone takes over new client intake process and sets pricing.
- Joint strategic meeting held to review first 6 months and adjust timeline.

Months 13–18: Leadership Cemented

- Simone is introduced as "Managing Partner" in all external communications.
- Staff trained to escalate concerns to Simone only.
- Alicia steps back from all client contact, except for one legacy client she personally managed.
- Business website updated with Simone's bio as lead owner.

Months 19–24: Final Transition + Exit

- Alicia informs clients she is stepping into retirement and expresses full confidence in Simone.
- Simone attends a regional conference on behalf of the business—a first.
- Alicia's email is removed from staff distribution lists.
- Final advisory lunch between Alicia and Simone to reflect and set goals for Year 3 and beyond.

What Made This Work

- **Written handoff schedule:** Both parties knew what was changing each quarter.
- **Clear client communication:** Clients weren't surprised—they were guided through it.
- **No shared authority:** Each responsibility had a defined handoff point. No limbo.
- **Emotional preparation:** Alicia took a short sabbatical in Month 20 to help herself detach.

This transition didn't just keep the business stable—**it helped it grow.** By Year 3, Simone had added two new client accounts and hired a fifth staff member. And Alicia, by her own words, was finally "on the beach with a book, not a balance sheet."

9

REAL CASE STUDIES (SUCCESSES & FAILURES)

SECTION 1: WHY CASE STUDIES MATTER

It's one thing to talk about internal succession in theory—spreadsheets, contracts, and timelines. But what really brings these strategies to life are the real stories of business owners who've walked the path. Some succeed brilliantly. Others struggle, stall, or fail. All of them leave behind critical lessons for the rest of us.

This chapter exists for one reason: to show you what internal succession actually looks like when real people try to pull it off.

You've probably noticed that most books about business succession stick to generic advice and hypothetical examples. That's not good enough. You need to see what works—and what blows up—so you can plan for both. Stories don't just make things easier to understand. They expose blind spots, validate your instincts, and give you a realistic benchmark.

The case studies in this chapter are all based on real businesses. In some cases, names and details have been changed to protect privacy. In others, elements from multiple businesses are combined into a single narrative to preserve anonymity while keeping the core lessons intact. These aren't meant to impress you—they're meant to inform you.

You'll read about:

- A clean, successful transfer to a key employee
- A more complicated transition between two internal successors that almost derailed
- A painful family succession that failed due to lack of structure and fit

These stories are here to help you ask better questions, write stronger contracts, and avoid the kinds of mistakes that can destroy even a profitable business. If you only take one thing from this chapter, let it be this: **Internal succession is never about luck. It's about structure, support, and strategic humility.**

SECTION 2: THREE CASE STUDIES

Case Study #1 – A Textbook Transition
Business Type: Mid-sized regional HVAC company
Successor: Longtime operations manager
Structure: Seller-financed buyout over seven years with profit-sharing
Transition Length: Three-year phased handoff

This case represents an ideal internal succession. The founder of a successful HVAC company had spent over 30 years building a loyal customer base and a stable team. With retirement on the horizon, he identified his operations manager—a 15-year veteran of the company—as the ideal successor. The manager had deep institutional knowledge, strong relationships with employees and vendors, and a clear desire to continue the company's legacy.

Rather than rushing the deal, the two parties created a structured transition plan that unfolded over three years. In Year One, the successor took over scheduling and field operations. In Year Two, he assumed responsibility for staffing and vendor contracts. By Year Three, he was managing the books, overseeing the P&L, and preparing for full ownership.

The deal was financed through a combination of seller financing and profit-sharing. The successor paid a small down payment and agreed to annual installments, with payments tied to net profits. This aligned both parties' incentives: the seller was motivated to support a strong transition, and the buyer had every reason to protect margins and manage growth responsibly.

Clear contractual terms helped avoid common pitfalls. A detailed operating agreement included:

- Defined handoff milestones
- A profit threshold below which payments could be deferred (a built-in pause clause)
- A clawback provision if gross revenue dropped by more than 25% for two consecutive years
- Step-in rights allowing the seller to temporarily resume control in case of material mismanagement

Throughout the transition, staff retention remained high and customer satisfaction scores remained stable. The outgoing owner retained a consulting role for one additional year, participating in strategic planning and serving as a steadying presence during the full ownership transfer.

This case illustrates the key elements of a successful internal transition:

- **Preparation:** Successor training began well before the formal transfer
- **Alignment:** The deal structure incentivized shared success
- **Documentation:** The contract addressed both opportunity and risk
- **Support:** The seller offered mentorship, not interference

Too often, succession is reactive. In this case, it was proactive, intentional, and structured—resulting in a stable handoff, long-term business continuity, and financial security for both parties.

Case Study #2 – A Risk That Paid Off

Business Type: Creative marketing agency
Successors: Two mid-level employees (co-managers)
Structure: Earn-out agreement with seller retaining 25% equity for two years
Transition Length: Two years, staggered responsibilities

This case illustrates a more complex internal succession involving multiple successors and an evolving ownership structure. The business, a boutique marketing agency with 18 employees, was known for its innovative campaigns and strong client relationships. The founder, facing burnout and eager to reduce day-to-day involvement, identified two promising mid-level employees to take over.

Neither successor had run a company before. However, each brought complementary strengths: one led the client services team and was known for her leadership skills, while the other excelled at creative direction and project delivery. After careful vetting, the founder agreed to a co-leadership succession plan, structured around a phased earn-out.

The deal involved a gradual shift in authority. In the first year, both successors were promoted to co-managing directors and began handling departmental budgets, client renewals, and hiring. By the second year, they were managing company strategy, investor reporting, and culture initiatives.

The ownership transfer was structured through an earn-out: the founder retained 25% equity for the first two years post-transition, receiving distributions based on profitability. The remaining 75% was transferred via seller financing, with payments tied to quarterly performance metrics. A clause in the agreement allowed the successors to buy out the remaining 25% after two years, provided the company hit agreed-upon revenue and EBITDA benchmarks.

(EBITDA stands for Earnings Before Interest, Taxes, Depreciation, and Amortization — a common measure of a business's operating performance and profitability.)

Despite a strong start, the transition encountered serious friction. The two successors disagreed on staffing priorities and had differing opinions about client acquisition strategy. The tension began to affect morale and led to the departure of several long-term employees.

To stabilize the business, an outside advisor was brought in. Acting as both coach and mediator, the advisor helped the successors define clearer roles and accountability metrics. The seller also extended his consulting involvement by six months to support the resolution process. Over time, the successors regained employee confidence and improved operational efficiency, though the company lost a year of momentum during the conflict.

Eventually, the successors met their performance benchmarks and completed the buyout. The founder exited with full payment and a legacy preserved. While the process was bumpier than anticipated, the structure of the deal—especially the phased authority, equity retention, and advisor involvement—helped preserve the company through a turbulent transition.

This case demonstrates that:
- **Shared leadership can work**, but only with clear roles and open communication
- **Advisor support can be critical** during friction points
- **Earn-out structures offer flexibility**, but also require contingency planning
- **Even imperfect transitions can succeed** if the framework is strong enough

Internal succession often requires adapting in real time. In this case, the risk of joint successors was mitigated through structure, outside support, and a commitment to long-term success.

Case Study #3: The Deal That Fell Apart
Business Type: Multi-location family-owned bakery
Successor: Founder's eldest daughter
Structure: No formal agreement; informal transition with verbal promises
Transition Length: Attempted handoff over 18 months, ultimately reversed

This case study illustrates how a lack of structure, unclear expectations, and unresolved personal dynamics can unravel even the best-intentioned internal succession plan.

The business was a well-loved regional bakery chain with four locations and a 40-year reputation for high-quality products. The founder, nearing 70 and facing health concerns, began stepping back from day-to-day operations. His eldest daughter, who had worked in the business off and on for two decades, was the presumed successor. She was popular with staff, knew many of the regular customers, and had a strong sentimental connection to the brand.

However, no formal succession plan was created. There was no written agreement, no updated operating procedures, and no clear financial model. The founder assumed his daughter would "take over when the time was right," and she assumed the business would one day be hers. Neither fully articulated expectations, timelines, or responsibilities.

In practice, this meant confusion from the start. Authority was never clearly transferred. Employees continued going to the founder with questions. Vendors didn't know who to contact. Financial reporting lagged. The founder criticized his daughter's decisions behind her back, and she increasingly resented his interference.

Without legal clarity, the daughter also had no ownership stake or protection. She began investing her own money into renovations and marketing campaigns, believing she was building her future — but the business still legally belonged to her father. When tensions escalated over hiring choices and cost control, their relationship deteriorated. Ultimately, the founder reversed course and announced that he was not ready to retire and would be bringing in an outside manager to "stabilize things."

The fallout was painful. The daughter resigned and opened a competing café a few miles away. Half the original staff followed her. Customers were divided. The bakery's revenue dropped 30% in the following year, and one location eventually closed. Meanwhile, the family relationship remains fractured.

This case highlights the critical importance of structure, even (and especially) in family transitions:

- **Verbal agreements aren't enough.** Good intentions can turn sour without legal clarity and documented expectations.
- **Ownership must be formalized.** Sweat equity only works when backed by enforceable rights.
- **Family dynamics require professional boundaries.** Even the closest relationships can be strained under unclear leadership.

In contrast to the structured deals in previous sections, this example shows how ambiguity, avoidance, and assumptions can destroy both a business and a family legacy. Internal succession only works when it's treated like the high-stakes business transaction it is—not an informal favor or inheritance.

SECTION 3: LESSONS ACROSS ALL CASES

Internal succession is never one-size-fits-all. But when you look across different industries, deal types, and personalities, certain patterns emerge—both in what drives success and what causes failure.

Here's what these three case studies reveal:

Structure is non-negotiable

The strongest transitions weren't necessarily the smoothest—they were the best-structured. Whether it was a solo successor or a co-leadership team, having a clear legal framework, defined milestones, and built-in contingencies created a shared roadmap. In contrast, the unstructured family handoff lacked guardrails and quickly went off-course.

Relationships matter, but they're not enough

Trust, loyalty, and shared history are essential—but they're not substitutes for accountability. In each successful case, relationships were reinforced by contracts, defined roles, and financial modeling. Where failure occurred, emotional bonds were expected to carry the weight of business responsibility. They couldn't.

Support is underrated

In the more complex transition, success hinged on external support: a business advisor who helped navigate friction and reset expectations. Even in the cleanest case, the seller stayed on in a consulting role to offer mentorship. Transitions don't happen in a vacuum—and solo successors rarely thrive without guidance.

Conflict doesn't equal failure

The co-leadership case was rocky, but it ultimately succeeded. The difference was that the team adapted, got help, and stayed focused on the goal. Conflict is inevitable. The question is whether the structure allows for recalibration and whether the parties are committed enough to make it work.

Delay is more dangerous than disagreement

In the failed family transition, the biggest mistake wasn't disagreement—it was avoidance. The founder and daughter delayed formal planning for years, assuming good intentions would be enough. By the time tension surfaced, it was too late to fix. The damage—to the business and the relationship—was done.

Across all three examples, the message is clear: internal succession is a leadership process, a legal transaction, and a human relationship. Get all three aligned, and you can pass the torch successfully. Ignore even one, and the flame might go out.

SECTION 4: RED FLAGS AND SUCCESS SIGNALS

Whether you're handing off your business or stepping into ownership, certain patterns should make you pause—or give you confidence. Below are the clearest **warning signs** and **green lights** that emerged from the case studies in this chapter.

Red Flags: Warning Signs Your Internal Succession Is at Risk

- **No written agreement:** If expectations, responsibilities, and financial terms aren't documented, you're building on quicksand.
- **Ambiguous roles:** When staff, clients, or even the successor don't know who's in charge, confusion will stall momentum and erode trust.
- **Deferred decision-making:** Postponing key discussions—about equity, control, compensation, or timelines—allows tension to fester unchecked.
- **Unclear or unmeasurable performance benchmarks:** If no one can say what success looks like, disputes are inevitable.
- **Overreliance on "gut feel":** Choosing a successor based on loyalty or familiarity without vetting their leadership capacity is a gamble — and often a costly one.
- **Family dynamics overshadowing business needs:** When emotional baggage dictates decision-making, objectivity suffers—and so does the company.

- **Resistance to outside input:** Refusing legal, financial, or strategic advice is often a sign that the transition is being driven by ego, not good governance.

Success Signals: Signs You're on the Right Track

- **Clear, time-bound transition phases:** A gradual handoff with measurable milestones creates accountability and builds confidence.
- **Legal and financial clarity:** Well-drafted contracts, operating agreements, and financing terms signal professionalism—and protect both parties.
- **Aligned incentives:** When buyer and seller benefit from the same outcomes (e.g., profit-sharing, earn-outs), they stay motivated to collaborate.
- **Mentorship without micromanagement:** Sellers who offer guidance without clinging to control set successors up to lead independently.
- **Role-specific support systems:** Advisors, consultants, or board members can help successors navigate the inevitable bumps in the road.
- **Cultural continuity:** When staff and clients remain loyal during the transition, it's a strong sign that leadership has transferred successfully.
- **Emotional maturity on both sides:** Succession works best when both parties can handle feedback, negotiate in good faith, and put the business first.

Recognizing these red flags and success signals early can help you adjust course before problems escalate. Internal succession is not just about choosing the right person—it's about setting them up to win.

SECTION 5: WHAT THIS MEANS FOR YOU

If you're serious about internal succession, you need more than a willing successor and a rough idea. You need a plan rooted in reality—one that accounts for the best-case scenario, the worst-case outcome, and everything in between.

The case studies in this chapter weren't chosen for drama. They were chosen because they reflect what actually happens inside small and mid-sized businesses when it's time to pass the torch. Some owners get it right from the beginning. Others adapt and recover. And a few lose what they spent a lifetime building.

Here's what to take with you:

- **Structure protects relationships.** If you want to preserve trust—especially with a family member or longtime employee—the best gift you can give them is a clear plan.
- **Success isn't automatic.** Even with the right person, transitions require coaching, legal support, and accountability. Don't assume desire equals readiness.
- **Failure is preventable.** Most failed transitions don't fall apart due to incompetence. They fall apart because of avoidance, assumptions, or a lack of follow-through.
- **You don't need to do this alone.** Advisors, consultants, and mentors can play a quiet but critical role. One well-timed conversation might prevent a costly mistake.

Most of all, don't wait until you're exhausted, ill, or burned out to start the conversation. Internal succession works best when it's driven by strength—not desperation. The sooner you begin planning, the more options you'll have, the stronger your successor will be, and the more likely your legacy will endure.

Now that you've seen what internal succession looks like in the real world, the next chapters will equip you to plan your own.

10

WHAT HAPPENS AFTER THE SALE

SECTION 1: THE SELLER'S NEW ROLE

Selling your business doesn't mean vanishing overnight—nor should it. In many internal succession deals, the seller transitions from being the primary operator to playing a support role during the handoff. This shift can be liberating, confusing, or even frustrating depending on how it's handled.

The key is intentionality. Just as you structured the deal and planned the transition, you also need to define your post-sale role with clarity and purpose. Otherwise, you risk becoming a shadow leader, a distraction to the new owner, or a source of resentment on both sides.

Here are the most common roles sellers step into after the deal—and the pitfalls to avoid with each.

1. The Advisor

In this scenario, the seller becomes a mentor or strategic advisor for a fixed period. You're available for regular check-ins, occasional decisions, or specific challenges, but you're not running the business day-to-day.

This is one of the most effective and healthy post-sale arrangements—when done correctly. It allows for:

- **Institutional knowledge transfer:** You can pass on lessons that aren't written down anywhere—vendor insights, client history, internal culture cues.
- **Crisis support:** When the successor hits a rough patch, you can offer guidance without judgment.
- **Emotional continuity:** Staff and clients see a familiar face, but one that's appropriately in the background.

What to avoid: The line between advisor and backseat driver is thin. If you're second-guessing decisions, attending every staff meeting, or making "suggestions" that feel like directives, you're undermining the very transition you worked so hard to build. If you promised to let go, let go—even if you see the new owner making a different (not necessarily wrong) choice.

2. The Consultant

Some sellers continue to offer post-sale consulting—and often, a certain number of consulting hours are included as part of the sale. This is especially common in small business deals where institutional knowledge, vendor relationships, and operational expertise don't easily transfer overnight.

In many cases:

- The buyer receives a set number of hours per month, included in the sale price, for a defined period (e.g., three to twelve months)
- A discounted consulting rate is agreed upon for additional hours or for work beyond that time frame
- Consulting services may be limited to specific areas—such as vendor transitions, lease negotiations, or seasonal planning

This arrangement provides continuity without placing the seller on the payroll and gives the buyer a reliable support system while building independence.

Some consulting relationships evolve over time into occasional, informal check-ins, particularly when the seller and buyer maintain a positive working relationship. These ongoing conversations can add value as long as boundaries are respected.

What to avoid: The key is balance. Consulting should be available, not automatic. If the successor starts relying on the seller to solve every problem, the handoff stalls. Likewise, the seller should avoid inserting themselves into situations unless asked—even if the business is headed in a different direction than they would have chosen.

The most successful transitions often involve a period of structured consulting, followed by a natural tapering-off as the new owner gains confidence and control.

3. The Silent Partner

In deals where the seller retains minority equity for a defined period, they may take on the role of silent partner—participating in profits but staying out of operations. This structure can keep the seller financially tied to the business while giving the new owner space to lead.

To make this work, the agreement must include:
- A clear operating agreement outlining decision rights
- Defined communication cadences (e.g., quarterly updates or board meetings)
- A shared understanding that the seller is not there to "veto" decisions unless specific triggers occur

What to avoid: Don't mistake equity for control. If you're no longer the majority owner or active operator, your role is to support from the sidelines—not to relitigate the handoff.

4. The Exit Artist

In some cases, the seller truly walks away. This is most common when:

- The buyer is fully prepared
- The seller has another venture or retirement plan ready to go
- The deal terms were clean, with little or no earn-out or equity retention

If structured properly, a full exit can be healthy for everyone involved. The seller departs with dignity, and the buyer steps into full authority from day one.

What to avoid: Avoid micromanaging from a distance. Checking in "just to see how things are going" too often, publicly commenting on company posts, or showing up at the office unannounced can signal to staff that the real power hasn't shifted—even if the paperwork says it has.

5. The Phantom Owner

This is the cautionary tale—he seller who appears to have exited, but hasn't truly let go. It's not always malicious. Sometimes it's subtle. But the result is the same: confusion, power struggles, and instability.

A Phantom Owner can appear in several ways:

- **Shadow approvals:** Staff continue checking with the seller "just to be safe"
- **Undermining authority:** The seller criticizes new decisions privately or offers contradictory guidance

- **Client interference:** Longtime customers are told, "You can always call me if anything changes"
- **Operational overreach:** The seller continues ordering supplies, managing vendors, or making scheduling decisions long after the transition begins

Sometimes this happens because control is being handed over gradually—a smart structure when done intentionally. But if the roles, responsibilities, and timeline aren't clearly mapped out, it's easy for lines to blur.

To prevent this, define a **transition calendar** with specific milestones:

Function	Final Day of Seller Control	Notes
Vendor orders	August 1	Buyer to assume ordering responsibilities
Lease and landlord relations	September 15	Buyer authorized to negotiate extensions
Employee raises & bonuses	October 31	Seller input ends after annual review
Payroll oversight	December 31	Buyer takes full control in January

This approach protects both parties:
- The buyer can gain confidence and competence over time
- The seller knows when to step back, and why
- The team knows who's in charge at each stage

What to avoid: Never assume that "we'll just figure it out" as you go. If you don't plan the exit, the exit won't happen—and the successor may forever operate in the seller's shadow. This creates resentment, ruins morale, and can even lead to the buyer walking away from the deal entirely.

The solution isn't silence—it's clarity. If the seller is staying involved in any capacity, document exactly how, when, and why. Then honor the agreement, even when it's difficult.

The Big Idea: Letting go isn't just about walking away. It's about choosing the right role for the new phase of your relationship with the business—and honoring that role with professionalism and restraint. Done well, your presence can be a stabilizing force. Done poorly, it can derail everything you've built.

SECTION 2: THE SUCCESSOR'S FIRST YEAR

The first year after an internal succession is both the most exciting and the most precarious. The business may look the same from the outside—same location, same staff, same customers—but internally, everything is shifting. A new owner is stepping into the spotlight, and with that comes responsibility, pressure, and the weight of expectations.

This is the moment where the deal stops being theoretical and becomes real. It's also the time when cracks in the transition plan tend to show up. Even a well-prepared successor can feel overwhelmed. And even the most supportive seller can struggle to step aside.

But handled with intention, the first year can solidify leadership, stabilize the organization, and set the tone for long-term success.

1. Establishing Authority

One of the biggest challenges for new owners is claiming legitimate authority—especially when the team already knows them in another role. This is especially true for successors who rose from within the organization. Yesterday, they were a peer or department lead. Today, they're the boss.

This can create tension:
- Employees may test boundaries to see what they can get away with
- Longtime staff may continue going to the seller for decisions
- Some team members may resist new processes or priorities
- The solution isn't to crack down—it's to communicate clearly.

The successor should:
- Hold a staff meeting early on to outline their vision, values, and expectations
- Reinforce their authority through action—making decisions, holding people accountable, and following through
- Avoid the temptation to make sweeping changes immediately unless there's an urgent need

Respect is earned through consistency. The more the team sees follow-through and decisiveness, the faster they adjust to the new leadership dynamic.

2. Managing Legacy Relationships

In many cases, the seller had deep personal relationships with clients, vendors, or senior staff—and the successor now inherits those relationships, along with the pressure to maintain them.

There's often an unspoken fear on both sides:
- **Clients** wonder: Will I get the same service?
- **Staff** wonder: Will this change how I'm treated or how decisions are made?
- **The Successor** wonders: Will I be accepted or compared?

Navigating this requires a delicate balance:
- Don't try to "be" the previous owner. Authenticity matters more than imitation.
- Schedule one-on-one meetings with key clients and vendors to build personal rapport.
- Acknowledge the past, but clearly frame the future. "Here's what we're continuing—and here's where we're evolving."

It also helps if the seller makes proactive introductions, explicitly communicates their confidence in the new owner, and redirects inquiries with statements like: "You'll want to ask [the successor]—they're the decision-maker now."

3. Building Systems and Confidence

Even if the successor already knew the business well, they'll now be responsible for areas they may not have handled directly before: legal matters, tax filings, insurance, vendor negotiations, or complex HR decisions. This can be daunting.

The most effective successors do three things:

1. **Create structure quickly.** Set up weekly staff meetings, implement reporting tools, and define key performance indicators (KPIs). Structure builds confidence—for the team and the new owner.
2. **Ask for help without shame.** Lean on the seller, advisors, or industry peers when needed. It's better to ask a question than to guess on legal or financial matters that carry long-term consequences.
3. **Track wins and progress.** Keep a running log of achievements in the first year—client renewals, efficiency improvements, successful hires, cost savings. It's a powerful morale booster and can serve as a confidence anchor when imposter syndrome creeps in.

4. Facing Inevitable Mistakes

Every successor makes mistakes. That's not a sign of failure—it's part of taking ownership.

Common first-year missteps include:

- Over-promising and under-delivering
- Being too quick to fire or too slow to act
- Micromanaging instead of delegating
- Failing to communicate during times of uncertainty

What matters isn't perfection—it's recovery. When a mistake happens:

- Own it quickly

- Correct it visibly
- Communicate transparently
- Learn from it systematically

Most teams will forgive a mistake far faster than they'll forgive inconsistency, defensiveness, or blame-shifting.

5. Balancing Vision and Continuity

New owners often walk a tightrope: they want to prove themselves by innovating, but they also need to preserve the aspects of the business that made it successful in the first place.

The most effective strategy is to **listen before leading change.** In the first year:

- Survey staff and customers to identify what's working—and what's not
- Maintain consistency in customer experience unless there's an urgent issue
- Choose **one or two visible improvements** to roll out—enough to show progress without overwhelming the team

Incremental change is easier to absorb—and easier to reverse if it misses the mark.

The Big Idea: The first year sets the tone for the rest of the journey. Success doesn't come from bold moves or radical change—it comes from clear communication, consistent leadership, and the willingness to grow into the role.

The new owner doesn't have to prove everything in the first 12 months. But they do have to earn trust, claim authority, and begin shaping the business in a way that reflects their leadership. That's how a handoff becomes a legacy.

SECTION 3: FINANCIAL TRANSITIONS

After the sale closes, the paperwork is signed, and the keys are handed over, there's often a quiet assumption that the financial side is now settled. In reality, this is just the beginning of a new financial relationship—one that requires vigilance, communication, and adaptability from both parties.

Internal succession deals typically involve ongoing financial obligations: installment payments, profit-sharing, consulting fees, or earn-outs. These moving parts can become points of friction if not managed clearly and proactively.

This section explores the key financial realities for both the **buyer** and the **seller** during the post-sale phase.

1. Managing Cash Flow While Paying Off the Deal

For the successor, the single biggest financial challenge in the first few years is **making payments to the seller while keeping the business stable**. If the purchase was seller-financed, every dollar of debt service must come from operating revenue—not outside investment.

To manage this successfully:

- **Create a rolling 12-month cash flow forecast.** Update it monthly. This allows the buyer to anticipate shortfalls and adjust spending early.
- **Build in a safety margin.** Don't operate on razor-thin margins hoping everything goes as planned. Assume there will be surprises—because there will.
- **Prioritize revenue protection.** Before cutting costs, protect the revenue engine: customer service, lead generation, and high-performing staff.

It's also wise to establish a reserve fund—even a modest one—to buffer against seasonal dips, client turnover, or economic downturns.

2. Clarifying the Seller's Income Stream

From the seller's perspective, the deal isn't "done" until payments are completed. Whether the structure includes monthly installments, profit-sharing, or equity distributions, the seller is relying on the business to perform well enough to meet its obligations.

This creates a unique dynamic: the seller no longer controls the business, but their financial future may still depend on it.

To protect their interests:

- The seller should receive **quarterly or monthly financial reports,** depending on the deal structure.
- There should be **clear consequences for late or missed payments,** including potential penalties or step-in rights, as outlined in the operating agreement.
- The parties should revisit the payment schedule annually and agree on any necessary adjustments, particularly in down years.

If the deal includes profit-based payments, both sides should agree on how "profit" is defined—typically using **EBITDA** (Earnings Before Interest, Taxes, Depreciation, and Amortization)—and how it's calculated.

Ambiguity in definitions is a common source of tension. Define everything up front—and revisit those definitions as the business evolves.

3. Setting Successor Compensation

In many cases, the successor becomes both owner and employee. That means they now need to draw a salary while also making payments to the seller and covering operating expenses.

This raises a key question: **How much should the new owner get paid in the early years?**

There's no one-size-fits-all answer, but guiding principles include:

- **The salary should be sustainable.** Paying themselves too much too soon can strain cash flow and jeopardize the deal.
- **The salary should reflect market norms.** Use industry benchmarks for someone in a comparable leadership role, adjusting for company size and geography.
- **Profit distributions can be delayed.** It's common for successors to hold off on taking distributions until the deal is further along or certain thresholds are met.

A well-written agreement often distinguishes between salary (as a paid employee) and profit distributions (as an owner). This protects the business while still allowing the successor to support themselves.

4. Tax Planning for Both Parties

Both the seller and the buyer need tailored tax guidance in the first few years post-sale.

For the **seller**, key issues include:
- **Capital gains tax** on the sale proceeds
- **Ordinary income tax** on consulting fees or ongoing payments
- **Installment sale reporting** over time, especially for seller-financed deals

For the **successor**, priorities include:
- **Proper payroll tax setup** if they're drawing a salary
- **Depreciation schedules** for purchased assets
- **Deductibility of interest** on loan payments or seller financing

Ideally, both parties will work with tax professionals who understand the deal structure and can coordinate to ensure consistent reporting. A misalignment in tax treatment can trigger audits or lead to unintended liabilities.

5. Renegotiating When Necessary

Not every transition goes according to plan. Revenue may dip. Expenses may spike. A key customer might leave. When that happens, it's important to remember that a well-structured deal doesn't just protect the seller—it also gives both sides a way to adapt.

Common financial renegotiations include:

- **Temporary payment pauses** if revenue falls below a defined threshold
- **Restructuring the payment schedule** to extend the term or adjust amounts
- **Switching from fixed to percentage-based payments** in unpredictable years

These changes should always be documented in writing, with updated signatures from both parties. Informal agreements or "handshake fixes" can unravel quickly—especially if the business continues to struggle or if ownership changes again in the future.

The Big Idea: Financial success after the sale depends less on hitting your targets perfectly and more on how well you manage through the inevitable fluctuations. Cash flow discipline, clear reporting, tax planning, and structured renegotiation options allow both buyer and seller to stay on the same page—even when business conditions change.

Money is one of the most sensitive parts of the post-sale relationship. Handle it with professionalism, transparency, and proactive planning, and it becomes a source of strength rather than stress.

SECTION 4: CULTURAL SHIFTS AND CONTINUITY

One of the most overlooked—and most fragile—parts of a business transition is **company culture.** Clients and employees may stay, processes may stay, and even the name on the door may stay. But if the culture changes too much, too fast—or in the wrong direction—the heart of the business can begin to fade.

Culture is not just "how we do things around here." It's how people feel about coming to work. It's how they make decisions when no one is watching. It's the stories people tell at lunch, the tone of internal communication, and how customers are treated when something goes wrong.

During the first year post-sale, culture is in motion—whether you acknowledge it or not.

1. Understanding What the Culture Is

Before making any cultural changes, the successor needs to understand the current culture deeply—not just from the seller's perspective, but from the inside out.

Ways to assess culture include:
- Anonymous employee surveys
- Exit interviews with departing staff
- One-on-one conversations across departments
- Customer feedback reviews

Ask questions like:
- What do we do well that you hope doesn't change?
- What frustrates you that no one seems to talk about?
- What's one thing you'd never want to lose here?

Understanding the culture doesn't mean preserving it in amber. It means identifying which parts are worth protecting—and which parts are ready for evolution.

2. Preserving What Works

When leadership changes, employees often brace for impact. They assume the new owner will bring in "their people," rewrite the handbook, or change core values. Even if that's not the intention, the anxiety can erode morale.

The best successors reassure early and often. Some effective strategies:

- Reaffirm core values and what will remain unchanged
- Publicly recognize team members who embody the existing culture
- Keep familiar rituals—like team lunches, internal shout-outs, or company traditions—in place, at least initially

Cultural continuity creates psychological safety. That, in turn, allows the team to stay focused on customers, results, and growth—not on protecting themselves.

3. Leading Intentional Change

Every business culture has blind spots—habits, norms, or power dynamics that may have gone unchallenged for years. The successor brings a fresh set of eyes, which can be a powerful opportunity to lead thoughtful change.

Key principles for shifting culture:

- **Start with why.** Change feels less threatening when people understand the reason behind it.
- **Involve your team.** Ask for input before rolling out new policies or systems.
- **Change one or two things at a time.** Too much change too quickly can trigger resistance or burnout.
- **Model the new behavior.** If you want a more collaborative, accountable, or creative culture, you must demonstrate it every day.

Change should feel like evolution, not upheaval. The team should still recognize the business six months after the sale—even as it grows stronger under new leadership.

4. Avoiding Culture Drift

Culture can drift when no one is paying attention. This often happens during long transitions, when roles are unclear or when neither the seller nor the buyer fully owns the tone and expectations.

Watch for these signs of cultural drift:
- Increased gossip or internal tension
- Decline in service quality or team morale
- Mixed messages about who's really in charge
- "That's not how we used to do it" becoming a frequent refrain

The solution is consistent communication. Use weekly meetings, one-on-ones, and even informal conversations to reinforce your expectations and listen to concerns. Culture needs constant tending, especially during times of change.

The Big Idea: Culture doesn't take care of itself. It either evolves by design—or unravels by accident. The most successful successors respect the culture they inherit, identify what makes it strong, and then carefully shape it to reflect their leadership values. Done well, this becomes the hidden engine that powers retention, trust, and long-term success.

SECTION 5: SHIFTING ROLES

1. The Seller's Emotional Journey

Letting go of control is rarely easy—especially when identity and legacy are tied to the business. Many sellers experience a mix of pride, anxiety, grief, and relief. The emotions don't follow a neat sequence. They can show up all at once or shift unexpectedly as the transition unfolds.

Common emotional responses include:

- **Pride and satisfaction:** Watching someone they trained take the reins successfully
- **Loss of relevance:** Feeling out of the loop or sidelined after years of being the decision-maker
- **Anxiety:** Worrying about whether the successor will maintain standards, treat employees well, or uphold the brand
- **Grief:** Mourning the end of a chapter that defined their working life

For many, retirement or exit isn't the goal—it's a confrontation with change. Sellers do best when they:

- Plan for their *next chapter* with intention (whether it's rest, travel, volunteerism, or new ventures)
- Create routines that maintain meaning and structure
- Stay socially connected, especially with peers or mentors who understand the experience of stepping back

And if they stay involved in the business in any role, it's critical that their participation is **well-defined**—both for their emotional well-being and the successor's confidence.

2. The Successor's Emotional Landscape

Taking over a business—especially from a mentor or family member—brings its own emotional challenges. Successors often face a blend of imposter syndrome, fear of disappointing others, and pressure to prove themselves.

Common emotional themes include:

- **Imposter syndrome:** "Am I really the right person for this?"
- **Fear of judgment:** "Everyone is watching to see if I mess up."
- **Over-identification:** Feeling responsible for fixing every problem immediately

- **Guilt or loyalty conflict:** Especially if changes upset staff or diverge from the founder's style

These emotions can cause a new owner to second-guess themselves, avoid difficult decisions, or overcompensate by asserting control too aggressively.

Successors benefit from:

- **Mentorship or peer support:** Talking with others who have gone through a similar transition
- **Professional coaching:** Especially in the first year, when leadership identity is still forming
- **Self-reflection:** Journaling, debriefing major decisions, or checking in with trusted advisors
- **Celebrating wins:** Taking time to acknowledge progress and growth

Ownership is a shift in identity—not just a change in job title. The faster a successor accepts the emotional weight of leadership, the faster they grow into the role.

3. Navigating Legacy Relationships

Transitions can create complicated emotions in the broader team, too—particularly among employees who had strong relationships with the seller.

Some common challenges:

- **Divided loyalty:** Employees may feel unsure whether to align with the old or new leadership style
- **Unresolved grief:** Especially if the seller was beloved or deeply involved in team culture
- **Uncertainty about the future:** "Will things change? Will my job change? Will I still be valued?"

To ease the emotional turbulence:

- The seller should offer a **clear and public endorsement** of the successor

- The successor should make space to **listen** to staff concerns without defensiveness
- Both parties should present a **unified front** during the transition period

Emotional clarity and transparency go a long way. Employees are remarkably adaptable—but they need to know that change isn't abandonment, and that their contributions still matter.

4. Conflict Is Normal

Even in the most amicable transitions, there will be moments of tension. Miscommunications, differing opinions, and unmet expectations are inevitable—especially when both parties care deeply about the business.

The goal isn't to avoid conflict entirely, but to navigate it with maturity and grace.

Key principles for handling emotional friction:
- **Use the contract as an anchor.** When in doubt, return to what was agreed upon.
- **Separate emotion from decision-making.** Vent in a safe space, but negotiate from a calm one.
- **Acknowledge the relationship.** Don't pretend it's "just business" if it's not. Respect the human side of the transition.
- **Don't triangulate.** Avoid dragging employees or customers into interpersonal disagreements.

Most emotional breakdowns during succession don't stem from the numbers—they stem from unspoken fears, mismatched expectations, or bruised egos. The cure is direct conversation, emotional intelligence, and occasionally, professional mediation.

The Big Idea: Business transitions are human transitions. The spreadsheets matter—but so do the stories, the fears, the pride, and the sense of loss or arrival that each person carries into the process. If the emotional landscape is acknowledged and navigated with care, the transition becomes more than a transaction. It becomes a rite of passage—one that honors the past while empowering the future.

SECTION 6: TOOLS FOR SUCCESS

After the ownership transition, it's easy to assume the hard part is over. But the first few years post-sale require just as much strategy and discipline as the deal itself. The difference is in focus: now it's about **sustaining momentum, empowering leadership, and building durable systems.**

The good news? You don't have to do it alone.

The most successful transitions rely on a handful of well-chosen tools—not just software or checklists, but structural supports that help both buyer and seller stay aligned, adapt when needed, and grow into their new roles.

1. Regular Check-Ins and Strategic Planning

Whether formal or informal, a structured cadence of check-ins between the seller and the successor is one of the simplest, most powerful tools in a successful transition.

This might include:
- **Monthly calls** during the first six months post-sale
- **Quarterly in-person strategy sessions**
- **A shared transition dashboard** with milestones, open issues, and financial updates

These check-ins prevent small issues from snowballing and give both parties a space to ask questions, clarify expectations, and course-correct if needed.

As the transition stabilizes, these meetings can taper off—but early on, they are essential to ensuring the deal isn't just completed on paper, but thriving in practice.

2. Outside Advisors and Coaches

An internal succession can feel isolating, especially for the successor. Even with the seller's support, the successor is now the one at the top—and sometimes that means making decisions with incomplete information, or under pressure, or while managing a steep learning curve.

That's where outside support makes all the difference.

Consider:

- **Executive coaches** who specialize in first-time leaders or family business transitions
- **Fractional CFOs or COOs** who can temporarily support the successor in technical areas
- **Peer mastermind groups** or local business roundtables

Sellers can benefit, too—especially when working through identity shifts or exploring new ventures. A good advisor helps keep emotions in check, focuses decisions, and provides a grounded outside perspective during moments of doubt or conflict.

3. Documentation and Knowledge Management

Much of what the seller knows lives in their head: vendor quirks, employee backstories, off-the-books workflows, past lessons from trial and error. If that knowledge isn't captured, it leaves with them—even if they're still loosely involved.

A few simple tools can make a big difference:

- A **centralized SOP library** (Standard Operating Procedures)
- **Recorded walkthroughs** of recurring processes or software systems

- A shared document outlining **key historical decisions,** including rationale and lessons learned

Transferring this "soft knowledge" is as important as the legal and financial documentation. It's what turns continuity into confidence.

4. Culture and Engagement Tracking

Culture can shift quickly after a transition, even with good intentions. Having tools in place to monitor team morale and engagement helps catch issues early—before they turn into turnover.

Options include:
- **Quarterly pulse surveys** (anonymous)
- **One-on-one listening sessions** during the first year
- **Clear feedback channels** like suggestion boxes or open-door policies

Some successors even use tools like CultureAmp or TinyPulse to automate this process. The key isn't the software—it's the follow-through. When staff feel heard and see action taken, trust builds.

5. Performance Metrics and Dashboards

Post-sale transitions are emotionally charged. Metrics provide an objective counterbalance—a way to track progress, identify red flags, and keep both parties aligned around business health.

Useful metrics may include:
- Monthly revenue and gross margin
- Customer retention and acquisition rates
- Staff turnover or absenteeism
- Successor-specific KPIs (e.g., collections, project delivery, vendor renewals)

Some deals even tie seller payments or earn-outs to these metrics. But even when they don't, having a shared dashboard gives both buyer and seller visibility into how the business is doing—and where to focus next.

6. A Written Transition Wrap-Up

At the one-year mark—or whatever timeline you define—the seller and successor should sit down for a **final transition review.** This can be formal or informal, but it should cover:

- What went well?
- What didn't?
- What's left to document, fix, or clarify?
- How do we handle contact going forward?

This wrap-up marks the shift from transition to independence. It also gives both parties a chance to close the chapter with clarity, dignity, and mutual respect.

The Big Idea: The most successful transitions don't rely on memory, emotion, or good intentions. They're supported by systems— consistent meetings, outside advisors, shared dashboards, cultural monitoring, and formal wrap-ups. These tools don't just manage the business. They protect the relationship—and that's what keeps the deal strong long after the ink is dry.

11

SPECIAL SCENARIOS

Not every internal succession follows a straight line. While earlier chapters have focused on deals where timing, financing, and readiness align, real-world transitions are rarely that tidy. This chapter addresses the outliers—the scenarios that require additional creativity, legal safeguards, or emotional support. Whether your successor isn't quite ready, your business has unique licensing requirements, or your family dynamics are anything but simple, thoughtful planning can still lead to a successful exit.

SECTION 1: WHEN THE SUCCESSOR ISN'T READY YET

One of the most common hurdles in internal succession is identifying a promising successor who simply isn't ready—yet. They may lack operational experience, management skills, or the confidence to lead. But walking away from a business you've built just because your ideal successor needs time would be a mistake. In many cases, it's possible to structure a transitional period that supports both continuity and growth.

Interim Leadership Models

If the owner needs to step back but the successor isn't prepared to step up fully, an interim leadership structure can provide stability. This might include hiring an experienced general manager, bringing in a fractional CEO, or forming a temporary advisory board. These options ensure day-to-day operations run smoothly while giving the successor time to build necessary skills and confidence.

Delayed Succession with Scheduled Benchmarks

Some transitions are best treated as a phased plan with clear benchmarks. Instead of a one-time sale, the owner might remain involved in a reduced role—such as overseeing financials or mentoring—while the successor gains hands-on experience. Progress should be tied to tangible metrics: revenue targets, staff retention, or successful completion of training programs. This builds accountability into the process and provides peace of mind for both parties.

How to Set Measurable Milestones

Vague goals like "become more confident in leadership" don't work in succession planning. Instead, set milestones such as:
- Completion of a management course or certification
- Leading a full budget cycle
- Successfully hiring and managing a team
- Running operations independently for 90 consecutive days

These milestones should be agreed upon in writing and tied to specific succession stages—such as increased equity, expanded authority, or a formal title change.

If the successor fails to meet agreed-upon milestones, the owner should retain the right to pause, adjust, or even reconsider the deal. A written performance framework isn't just for the successor—it protects the seller's interests too.

SECTION 2: FAMILY CONFLICTS OR UNEQUAL HEIR INTEREST

Passing a business to the next generation can be deeply rewarding—or devastatingly divisive. Family dynamics complicate succession planning more than any other variable. One child may have worked in the business for years, while another pursued a different path. Some may want ownership without responsibility; others may want control without experience. The goal isn't always equal treatment—it's fair treatment, and those aren't the same thing.

Active vs. Inactive Heirs

When one child has been instrumental in building the business and the others have not, a direct split in ownership can create resentment on both sides. The active heir may feel undermined or unsupported. The inactive heirs may feel excluded or financially shortchanged.

One common solution is to give the business to the active heir and offset it with other assets—real estate, investments, or life insurance—for the rest of the family. If equal asset distribution isn't possible, the inactive heirs may receive a promissory note tied to business performance, giving them a payout over time without compromising the successor's control.

Equal vs. Equitable

Equality assumes everyone gets the same. Equity considers contribution, risk, and future responsibility. A founder may decide it's more equitable to give full ownership to one child who has committed their career to the company, rather than forcing shared control among siblings who aren't involved. Documenting this decision in a clear, legally binding way is essential. An unclear or informal succession plan often leads to years of legal battles and damaged relationships.

Using Trusts or Buyout Agreements

To reduce family friction, some owners place the business in a trust with a designated trustee (often the successor) who is legally required to act in the best interest of all beneficiaries. This structure can protect the business from interference by uninterested parties while ensuring passive heirs receive distributions.

Alternatively, a buy-sell agreement can be used to allow one heir to purchase shares from the others over time. The terms of that agreement—including price, timeline, and funding source—should be defined well in advance, ideally while the founder is still involved to mediate any concerns.

When Emotions Run High

Even the best financial plans can unravel if the emotional dynamics aren't addressed. In cases where family tensions run deep or old grievances resurface, bringing in a neutral third party—such as a succession coach, mediator, or family business consultant—can help keep discussions productive and focused. In more complex or emotionally charged situations, family therapy may be appropriate. The goal is to create an environment where everyone feels heard, but the business still has a clear path forward.

SECTION 3: SUCCESSORS WITH LIMITED CAPITAL OR CREDIT

Internal succession often appeals to small business owners because it avoids the complexities of an outside sale. But many internal candidates—especially younger employees or family members— don't have the cash or credit to buy a business outright. Fortunately, limited capital doesn't have to be a deal-breaker. With the right structure, even financially constrained successors can complete a purchase over time, while protecting the seller's long-term interests.

Seller Financing with Contingency Protections

Seller financing is the most common solution in these scenarios. The founder agrees to accept payments over a set period—often five to ten years—rather than requiring a lump sum at closing. This approach makes the purchase accessible and allows the business itself to fund the deal.

However, extended payment timelines expose the seller to risk. To mitigate this, the deal should include protective clauses:
- **Clawbacks** if performance falls below agreed benchmarks
- **Security interests** in business assets or stock
- **Reversion clauses** that return control if default occurs

These legal protections ensure that if the buyer can't meet their obligations, the seller can recover ownership or receive compensation before the business deteriorates.

Gradual Buy-Ins Tied to Performance

In some cases, a full transfer isn't feasible from day one. A gradual buy-in can align ownership increases with demonstrated performance. For example:
- 10% ownership after managing operations for 12 months
- 25% after meeting net income targets
- 51% only after full repayment of an agreed base price

This stepwise approach ensures the successor earns equity over time, building both confidence and credibility with staff, clients, and lenders.

These arrangements should be formally documented and updated annually to reflect progress. Clear agreements help prevent misunderstandings and reinforce accountability.

Outside Investors or SBA Support as a Bridge

If seller financing alone won't bridge the gap, it may be worth bringing in a third-party investor or lender. While many founders are reluctant to involve outsiders in internal successions, a well-structured deal can still preserve majority control for the successor.

For instance, an SBA 7(a) loan allows a qualifying successor to borrow up to $5 million, which can cover a significant portion of the purchase price. The founder can carry a secondary note for the remainder. In some cases, a private investor may be willing to contribute capital in exchange for a minority stake, with a plan for the successor to buy them out later.

These options introduce complexity, but they can dramatically expand what's possible—especially for successors who are strong operators but don't have deep pockets.

SECTION 4: BUSINESSES WITH REGULATORY OR LICENSING ISSUES

Some businesses can't simply be handed over with a signature and a handshake. Industries with professional licensing, government oversight, or specialized certifications require careful planning to ensure a smooth transition. If the successor doesn't hold the necessary license—or can't obtain it in time—the entire deal can collapse or stall indefinitely.

Licenses That Don't Transfer

In certain industries, the license is issued to the individual, not the business entity. Law firms, medical clinics, accounting practices, and some financial services firms fall into this category. A business can't legally operate under new ownership unless the successor holds the correct license or the proper structure is put in place to comply with the law.

In these cases, succession might involve:

- A temporary **employment agreement** where the owner remains listed as the license-holder
- A **co-ownership model** where the licensed founder retains a minority stake until the successor is qualified
- A **management services agreement (MSA)** where the successor runs the business operations while the licensed individual remains responsible for compliance

These structures must be carefully reviewed by legal counsel to ensure they meet both regulatory requirements and ethical guidelines.

Planning Around Professional Designations

In some fields, licenses or credentials take years to obtain. For example, it may take two to three years for a successor to earn a CPA or veterinary license. In these cases, a long-range plan is essential.

Founders should:
- Identify qualified successors early and confirm their willingness to pursue licensing
- Support educational or training costs if needed
- Use interim structures (such as partnerships or apprenticeships) to bridge the gap

A delayed timeline doesn't mean the deal can't happen—it just means it needs a staged approach and a clear legal roadmap.

Succession Under Regulatory Scrutiny

Some businesses are subject to regulatory approval before a sale or change of control can occur. This is common in industries like banking, utilities, or defense contracting. If this applies, the deal must include:
- **Contingency clauses** based on agency approval
- **Timelines for application and review**
- A **backup plan** if the approval is denied or delayed

The more regulated the business, the more critical it is to bring legal and compliance experts into the succession process early. In many cases, a few months of advance planning can prevent years of delays—or worse, noncompliance penalties.

SECTION 5: KEY PERSON RISK AND CLIENT DEPENDENCY

In some small businesses, the founder isn't just the owner—they *are* the business. Their name is on the sign, their relationships drive revenue, and their presence reassures clients. This creates what's known as **key person risk**—when the value of the business depends disproportionately on a single individual.

If clients, vendors, or employees see the owner as irreplaceable, even a well-planned internal succession can falter. That's why mitigating key person risk is one of the most critical steps in preparing for a successful exit.

Transferring Trust, Not Just Control

Clients need to believe the business will continue to serve them with the same level of quality, care, and consistency after the owner leaves. That belief isn't built overnight.

A strong transition plan includes:

- **Gradually introducing the successor** as a decision-maker while the owner is still involved
- **Co-hosting client meetings, events, or calls** to build familiarity
- **Public messaging** (email newsletters, social media, website updates) that positions the successor as the natural next leader

The goal is to transfer trust over time, not in a single announcement. If clients know the successor, see their competence, and feel continuity, they're far more likely to stay.

Systematizing the Business

When the business revolves around the founder's personal knowledge or style, it can't easily be transferred. To reduce this risk:

- Document key processes in writing (sales, hiring, fulfillment, billing)
- Train multiple team members in essential functions
- Remove bottlenecks where only the founder has access or authority

If every important decision runs through one person, the business can't scale—or survive succession. A well-systematized company is far more resilient and valuable.

Branding Beyond the Founder

Sometimes even the business name creates dependency. If the company is called "John Martin Consulting," it may be harder for clients to trust someone who isn't John Martin.

In these cases, a **light rebrand** can help. Renaming the business to **JM Consulting** or **JMC** retains brand recognition while reducing the focus on one individual. It signals continuity without creating confusion—and it opens the door for new leadership to be seen as equally legitimate.

If a rebrand isn't feasible, reinforce the idea that the business is a *team*—not a one-man show. Update marketing materials to reflect collective expertise, showcase team members, and share client success stories led by others.

SECTION 6: THE PASSIVE OWNER MODEL

Not every successor wants to be in the trenches. Some buyers are interested in the business as a financial asset rather than a full-time job. This is especially common when the successor already owns other businesses or has a different primary profession. In these cases, the buyer becomes a passive owner—someone who holds the equity, reaps the profits, and delegates daily operations to a manager or team.

This model can work well, but only with the right infrastructure in place. Without careful planning, a passive owner structure can result in unclear leadership, falling performance, and loss of accountability.

Hire the Right Operator

The success of a passive ownership model depends almost entirely on the person running the business day-to-day. Whether it's an internal promotion or an external hire, this individual needs more than industry experience—they need business acumen, integrity, and a strong sense of ownership.

Clear expectations must be set around:
- Reporting structure
- Financial transparency
- Decision-making authority
- Key performance indicators (KPIs)

Consider using a written operating agreement that defines the manager's role, performance benchmarks, and consequences for underperformance.

Oversight Without Micromanagement

Passive owners should expect monthly or quarterly reporting on both financial and operational performance. Cloud-based accounting, scheduling, payroll, and CRM tools make it easier than ever to monitor from afar. Still, nothing replaces the occasional on-site visit to take the temperature of the culture.

Some owners also use performance-based bonuses or profit-sharing to incentivize their operators. When structured properly, these systems align interests and reduce the need for hands-on involvement.

SECTION 7: REMOTE OR PART-TIME SUCCESSORS

In some succession deals, the buyer lives out of state, is caring for a relative, or maintains a second job. While they may be capable and committed, they simply can't be physically present or fully available to the business.

This can work—but it introduces risk.

The Risk of Divided Focus

If the successor's attention is split, things can fall through the cracks. Vendors might not get paid. Staff morale may suffer. Opportunities for growth could be missed. The seller must carefully assess whether the business has the structure and staff to function without daily involvement from the new owner.

Some questions to ask:
- Who will manage the team, customers, and vendors day to day?
- Is there already a reliable second-in-command?
- Will the successor be reachable when issues arise?

If the answer to these questions isn't clear, consider including transition milestones in the deal structure. For example: requiring the successor to attend quarterly planning meetings in person, or limiting absentee ownership to the first year.

When to Say No

If the business is small, staff is lean, and the founder has always been the hub of all activity, a part-time successor is unlikely to succeed. In those cases, a phased buy-in or advisory role might be more appropriate—at least initially.

SECTION 8: SUCCESSOR IS A GROUP OR PARTNERSHIP

Sometimes a business is sold to a team rather than an individual—siblings, coworkers, friends, or a group of employees joining forces to take over. On paper, this can look like a dream team: complementary skills, shared history, and a unified vision. But in reality, group dynamics can be volatile, especially in the high-stress environment of a small business.

There's an old saying: **"The only ship that doesn't sail is a partnership."** While not always true, it serves as a sharp warning. Small business partnerships often fracture over disagreements about money, power, or work ethic. What begins as a unified front can quickly unravel when tough decisions need to be made, or when one partner feels they are carrying more of the load.

Decision-Making by Committee

When multiple people share ownership, **governance must be crystal clear.** Equal ownership with equal say may sound fair, but it can lead to gridlock. Sellers must think twice before handing their life's work—and their retirement income stream—to a committee with no tie-breaker or leader.

Key questions to resolve before closing the deal:
- Who has final say on key decisions?
- What happens if the partners disagree?
- Is there a designated managing partner, or rotating leadership?

If you're financing the sale, the business's continued performance directly affects your retirement. One falling out between partners could put your payments at risk. **This is not a time to rely on good intentions or verbal agreements.**

Structuring for Survival

Any group-buy succession plan should include:

- A detailed **operating agreement** or **shareholders' agreement**
- Defined **roles and responsibilities**
- **Tie-breaker provisions** and dispute resolution mechanisms
- A **buy-sell clause** in case one party wants to exit
- A clear path for how future equity decisions will be made

It's especially important to address imbalance. If one partner is investing more capital and another more time, make sure the ownership and compensation structure reflects that. Resentment festers quickly when effort and reward don't align.

As the seller, don't be afraid to **require a single point of contact** post-sale—someone responsible for reporting, payments, and ongoing communication. This helps avoid confusion and ensures continuity, even if there's internal drama among the new owners.

Know When to Say No

Selling to a group can work beautifully, but it carries real risk. If the group is loosely organized, untested in business decision-making, or avoiding hard conversations about control and compensation, you may be better off pursuing a different buyer—or requiring a trial period with phased ownership.

When your financial future depends on the next person—or people—running your business, caution is not just reasonable. It's essential.

SECTION 9: WHAT IF THE TRANSITION FAILS?

Despite everyone's best efforts, not every succession plan works. Sometimes the new owner struggles. Sometimes market conditions shift unexpectedly. Sometimes it becomes clear the wrong person took over. The key is not to prevent every possible failure—it's to plan for how you'll respond if things unravel.

A good succession agreement includes a "break glass in case of emergency" section that spells out exactly what happens if the business falters under new leadership.

Step-In Provisions

In seller-financed deals, one powerful protection is the right to **step back in and resume control** if the business is in serious trouble—financially or operationally. This must be written into the promissory note or sale agreement, along with the exact conditions that trigger it (e.g., missed payments, revenue declines, licensing issues).

Clawbacks and Resale Rights

Some sellers include **clawback clauses** that allow them to reclaim part of the business or reduce the remaining purchase price if key metrics aren't met. Others retain **resale rights:** the ability to find a new buyer and terminate the deal if things go off the rails.

The goal isn't to create an adversarial tone. It's to **protect the seller, the employees, and the legacy of the business** if the new leadership can't deliver.

Real-World Examples

Case #1: The Auto Shop Repossession—Fresno, California

Business: Joe's Complete Auto Care

Original Owner: Joe Ramirez, 62

Successor: A former employee with minimal management experience

Joe agreed to sell his busy six-bay auto repair shop to one of his longtime mechanics, financing 90% of the $650,000 sale over 7 years. The buyer knew cars but struggled with payroll, bookkeeping, and scheduling. Within 18 months, the shop was consistently behind on supplier bills, had bounced two payroll checks, and missed two consecutive payments to Joe.

Fortunately, Joe's agreement included a step-in clause that allowed him to **retake control if the buyer missed more than one payment or received two or more vendor complaints.** Joe resumed control of the business, kept the name, and rehired key staff. He eventually sold the shop to a local franchisee at a reduced price but recouped most of his equity.

Case #2: The Bakery That Went Cold—Portland, Maine

Business: Sweet Bay Baking Co.
Original Owner: Erin Cavanaugh, 55
Successor: A mother-daughter team from out of state

Sweet Bay had a loyal following and strong community roots. Erin accepted an offer from a mother and adult daughter who had dreams of running a bakery but little food service experience. The deal was cash up front for half the price and a three-year seller-financed balance, with Erin staying on as a consultant for six months.

Sales dropped within weeks. The new owners changed the menu, alienated staff, and ignored Erin's advice. By month five, customer traffic had plummeted, and by month eight, Erin stopped receiving payments. Her agreement included **no resale rights or step-in clause**—a costly mistake.

The buyers eventually abandoned the location, leaving Erin with a legal mess and an unpaid loan. She was forced to pursue litigation and later sold the building to another business. She now speaks openly about her experience, warning owners not to "confuse charm for competence."

Case #3: The IT Firm's Quiet Collapse—Chicago, Illinois

Business: BrightPoint Systems (small managed IT firm)
Original Owner: Darnell Hughes, 60
Successor: A promising young tech entrepreneur with investor backing

BrightPoint had built a solid recurring revenue model with 30 small business clients and five employees. The buyer offered a $1.2M purchase price with $600,000 down and the rest in performance-based payments over five years.

Darnell negotiated a **clawback provision:** if gross revenue dropped more than 20% in any two-year period, he would reclaim 15% of the business or reduce the remaining note by $200,000.

The successor aggressively cut support staff and shifted marketing focus, losing several key accounts. Revenue declined 23% by the end of year two. Darnell enforced the clawback clause, reducing the remaining note. The business stabilized but never regained its prior strength.

These examples show that **even the best-laid plans can fall apart**—but a solid legal framework can protect your interests and give you leverage when things go wrong. Hope is not a strategy. Protections like **step-in rights, clawbacks, and resale triggers** are the business equivalent of a seatbelt: you may not need them—but if you do, you'll be glad they're there.

SECTION 10: CONTINGENCY PLANNING FOR A FAILED TRANSITION

A failed transition doesn't just hurt the buyer—it can be devastating for the seller. In many internal succession deals, especially those involving seller financing, the former owner's **retirement income, financial security, and reputation** are tied directly to the business's ongoing success.

That's why smart succession agreements always include a **Plan B.**

Contingency planning doesn't mean you expect the buyer to fail. It means you've built protections in case something goes wrong— whether it's mismanagement, personal crisis, market downturn, or a simple mismatch between the buyer's skills and the business's needs.

Step-In Rights

One of the most powerful contingency tools is a **step-in clause,** which gives the seller the right to **retake control of the business** under clearly defined circumstances—such as missed payments, major operational failures, or serious revenue declines.

To be effective, this must be written into the promissory note or purchase agreement with precise triggers, like:

- Two or more missed payments
- A 25% drop in revenue for two consecutive quarters
- Major legal, licensing, or compliance violations

This gives the seller a way to protect the business—and the deal—without going to court.

Clawback Clauses Explained

Clawbacks allow the seller to **reduce the outstanding purchase price** or reclaim a portion of the business **if performance materially declines.** At first glance, this might seem like the seller is simply agreeing to accept less money. But in reality, it's a **risk-management tool** that can prevent much larger losses.

Let's walk through a practical example.

Example:

You sell your business for **$1 million**:
- $400,000 paid upfront
- $600,000 paid over 5 years (seller-financed)

The price assumes the business will continue earning **$500,000 in annual gross revenue**. But by year two, under new ownership, revenue has dropped to **$300,000** due to mismanagement. The buyer is struggling to make payments—and you're now financing a weaker, less valuable business than you agreed to.

If the buyer defaults, you might recover nothing.

With a clawback clause, the deal could include terms like:

"If gross revenue declines more than 25% over two consecutive quarters, the remaining loan balance is reduced by $100,000."

In this scenario, rather than defaulting, the buyer continues to pay a lower remaining balance—and you avoid a legal battle or complete collapse. You still collect income, protect your reputation, and retain leverage in the deal.

Clawbacks are especially useful when performance is difficult to guarantee. They create a **pressure-release valve**—adjusting the deal if the business underperforms, rather than letting the entire structure fall apart.

Resale Rights

In extreme cases, the best option is to unwind the deal and sell the business to someone else. **Resale rights** allow the seller to terminate the agreement and re-market the business if specific conditions aren't met. In some versions of this clause, the original buyer is refunded a portion of their investment—allowing a clean exit for both parties.

This is most commonly used when the business is losing money and no longer able to support the terms of the deal, or when the buyer is no longer engaged or reachable.

Mediation and Arbitration Clauses

Finally, contingency planning should include a **clear dispute resolution process.** Lawsuits are expensive and slow. Including a

mandatory mediation or arbitration clause ensures that if tensions rise, both parties are required to attempt resolution outside of court first. This protects everyone from legal escalation and creates space for renegotiation when necessary.

Extension of Term (When Cash Flow Slows Down)

In some cases, the buyer may not default—but cash flow may simply not support the agreed-upon timeline. This is especially true in slower growth businesses or during an economic downturn. Rather than forcing a default or missing payments, the seller and buyer may agree to **extend the term of the deal**—from, say, eight years to ten.

This keeps the payments manageable for the buyer while ensuring the seller continues to receive income—albeit on a longer timeline.

To protect both parties, the agreement should include:

- A **maximum allowable term** (e.g., "the full purchase price must be paid within 10 years, under all circumstances")
- A clear **approval process** for initiating an extension (often requiring written notice and supporting financials)
- Optional interest rate adjustments or minimum annual payments during the extension period

This option works best when the business is still healthy, the relationship is intact, and both parties are invested in the long-term success of the arrangement.

A Final Word

A well-written contingency plan doesn't signal distrust—it signals **professionalism and clarity.** Just as commercial leases have default clauses and banks demand collateral, a succession agreement should anticipate what might go wrong and outline how it will be handled.

If the business thrives, you'll never need these clauses.

But if it stumbles, you'll be glad they're there.

12

Final Thoughts
and Next Steps

SECTION 1: THE RISK OF DOING NOTHING

There is no neutral path when it comes to succession. Every small business owner is moving—consciously or not—toward a future where they will either exit on their terms or be forced out by time, illness, burnout, or death. The myth of "I'll just keep going" is comforting, but ultimately false. Aging out of your role is not an *if*—it's a *when*. And yet, far too many small business owners ignore this reality until it's too late.

The risk of doing nothing isn't just theoretical. It plays out every day in businesses across the country: the landscaping company that shuts down after 30 years because the owner never built a team that could function without him. The retail shop that closes abruptly when the owner has a stroke and no one knows where the vendor accounts or customer list is stored. The service business that quietly disappears when the founder retires and assumes a buyer will magically appear. Spoiler: they rarely do.

That fantasy—that someone will just show up one day with a check and an easy exit strategy—is one of the most dangerous myths in small business ownership. You've likely been told that if you build something good enough, someone will come along and buy it. But the reality is this: **there is no angel investor coming to save you.** No private equity firm is hunting for modestly profitable Main Street businesses. No cash-flush buyer is stalking your Yelp page waiting to pounce.

Most small businesses, if they sell at all, sell to someone already inside the business. An employee. A manager. A family member. Someone who already understands the value of what's been built—but only if you help them see the path to ownership.

Failing to plan isn't passive. It's an active decision—with consequences.

Without a succession plan, your business becomes a **liability** to your family instead of an asset. Your employees are left in limbo. Your clients or customers scatter. And the years of sweat equity you've poured into building something real? They evaporate faster than you think. No one's coming to rescue your business if you're no longer around to run it—and by the time your spouse or children are scrambling through old spreadsheets or fielding cold calls from bargain hunters, it's too late.

Even if the worst-case scenario doesn't occur, procrastination still costs you. The longer you wait to plan, the fewer options you have. A strong successor might leave for another opportunity. Your business may lose value as trends shift or your energy declines. You may end up taking a rushed deal with bad terms just to get out under pressure.

And perhaps most importantly, doing nothing robs you of peace of mind. As long as there's no plan, there's a lingering tension—like a storm you're pretending won't arrive. You may push it to the back of your mind, but it's there every time you think about getting older, needing a break, or wondering what happens if you get sick.

This book has been about more than structuring a deal. It's been about reclaiming control over your future. Succession planning is hard work. It forces you to make decisions you've avoided, confront fears you've buried, and have conversations you might not feel ready to have. But the alternative is worse: being caught off guard and leaving a mess for the people you care about most.

The bottom line is this: **no one regrets starting succession planning too early.** Many regret starting too late.

You've made it this far. You're no longer unaware or uninformed. Now the question is: **Will you take action?**

SECTION 2: YOU DON'T NEED A PERFECT PLAN— YOU NEED A START

Perfectionism is the silent killer of succession planning. It's easy to get caught in the trap of waiting until you have every piece figured out—the ideal successor, the perfect legal structure, a polished valuation, and a five-year timeline wrapped in a bow. But here's the truth: **you don't need a perfect plan—you need a start.**

Internal succession doesn't happen all at once. It's not a transaction—it's a process. And like any process, it gains clarity and momentum as you move forward. The first steps don't have to be big. They just have to be deliberate.

You might not know who your successor is yet. You might not be sure whether they're ready, or if you're ready. That's okay. The process begins with curiosity and exploration, not certainty. What matters most is that you start asking the right questions:

- If I had to leave the business tomorrow, who would I trust to run it?

- If that person isn't ready, could they be ready in two or three years?
- What would need to be true for this business to thrive without me?

These aren't theoretical questions. They're foundational. And the sooner you start thinking about them, the more options you'll have.

Too many business owners delay succession planning because they feel overwhelmed by complexity. They think they need a team of lawyers, accountants, and consultants just to begin. But most of the real work at the beginning is **emotional and strategic**, not legal. It's about mindset, not documents.

It starts with a conversation—with your spouse, your business partner, your top employee, or your own reflection in the mirror. It starts when you stop treating succession as something to be dealt with "someday" and start treating it as part of your job today.

In fact, one of the advantages of internal succession is that you can **test ideas in real time.** You can give someone more responsibility and see how they handle it. You can explore different deal terms without committing to them. You can build toward a transition gradually, adjusting as you go. That kind of flexibility is impossible once you list the business for sale on the open market or start taking meetings with brokers.

The other myth that slows people down is the idea that once you start succession planning, you're committing to leave. You're not. Starting the process doesn't mean you're stepping away tomorrow—it means you're protecting your future. In fact, most internal transitions take **three to five years** to complete. You'll have time to pivot, renegotiate, or pause if needed.

But none of that happens until you take the first step.

The perfect plan doesn't exist. Market conditions change. People change. Businesses evolve. But a good plan—one built on clarity, communication, and flexibility—can survive those changes. It can adapt. And it can give you peace of mind knowing you're moving toward a future where you're not chained to your business, or risking everything you've built by doing nothing.

If you've made it this far in the book, you're ready. Not ready to sell tomorrow, maybe. But ready to take control. Ready to think about life after ownership. Ready to protect the people who rely on your business. Ready to begin.

All you need now is the willingness to take the first small, imperfect step.

SECTION 3: A 12-MONTH ACTION ROADMAP

Succession planning can feel overwhelming—especially when you don't know where to begin. One way to cut through the paralysis is to break it into manageable pieces. You don't need to figure everything out at once. You just need a clear roadmap and a willingness to move one step at a time.

This 12-month framework isn't rigid, and it doesn't require perfection. But if you follow it, even loosely, you'll make meaningful progress toward protecting your business, your legacy, and your future.

Quarter 1: Define the Vision and Identify Key People

Goals:
- Define what you want from your eventual exit
- Identify potential successors
- Begin thinking about timing and deal structure

Action Steps:

- Block off time to reflect on your ideal retirement, lifestyle, and timeline
- Make a list of people already inside your business who could be successors
- If you don't have anyone in-house, consider whether a relative, manager, or partner might be trainable—or whether you'll need to recruit someone
- Start a folder or digital workspace to capture your thoughts, documents, and insights

This quarter is about **getting clear on what you want**, not committing to anything yet. If you have a partner or spouse, talk with them about your goals. If you're solo, consider hiring a coach or mentor to help you think it through.

Quarter 2: Test the Fit and Gather the Data

Goals:

- Begin informal conversations with your likely successor(s)
- Gather financials and operational data
- Test readiness and interest on both sides

Action Steps:

- Sit down with your potential successor and talk through your vision
- Be transparent: you're not making promises yet, but you are thinking about the future
- Review your books: P&L, balance sheet, cash flow, major contracts, debt
- Start documenting key processes and responsibilities if you haven't already
- Watch how your potential successor responds to increased responsibility or visibility

This quarter is about **exploration and alignment.** If your successor seems unsure or hesitant, don't panic. This is the time to surface doubts and clarify expectations—before lawyers and contracts get involved.

Quarter 3: Structure the Deal and Assemble Your Team

Goals:
- Begin outlining possible deal terms
- Start working with advisors
- Continue gradual delegation to the successor

Action Steps:
- Draft a preliminary outline of the deal: price range, payment terms, timeline, contingencies
- Consult a CPA or business-savvy financial advisor to test feasibility
- Bring in an attorney with experience in small business succession
- Explore tax implications of different structures (installment sale, partial buy-in, etc.)
- Delegate one or two core responsibilities to your successor and observe performance

This is where theory starts turning into action. You're not signing contracts yet, but you're getting closer. The people you bring onto your advisory team now will shape the tone and quality of the final deal.

Quarter 4: Formalize the Transition Plan and Set a Timeline

Goals:
- Lock in the structure
- Begin legal documentation
- Create a 2–3 year implementation timeline

Action Steps:

- Work with your attorney to draft the actual deal documents
- Identify specific benchmarks: when ownership will transfer, how performance will be measured, and what triggers clawbacks or step-in rights
- Create a communication plan: how and when to tell staff, clients, vendors
- Schedule quarterly check-ins for the next 12–24 months
- Consider a soft transition: gradually reducing your hours, shifting roles, or taking periodic sabbaticals

This is the most energizing and emotionally complex part of the process. You're beginning to **step back**—not all at once, but intentionally. At the end of this quarter, you should have a fully negotiated plan with target dates, signed documents, and a shared vision for the road ahead.

Final Thought

This 12-month roadmap won't look the same for every business. You may move faster or slower, skip a step, or spend extra time in one phase. That's okay. What matters most is that you're moving.

Internal succession is not a transaction—it's a transformation. And like any transformation, it takes time, intention, and a willingness to let go of total control in favor of long-term security.

You don't need to have every answer. You just need a plan—and now you have one.

SECTION 4: COMMUNICATION IS EVERYTHING

You can have the best deal structure, the cleanest financials, and the most qualified successor—but if your communication breaks down, your succession plan is at risk. At its core, internal succession is a human process. It involves trust, emotion, ego, and identity. And nothing derails it faster than poor communication.

Owners often delay or soften succession conversations out of fear: fear of destabilizing their staff, upsetting family members, or losing credibility with clients. But secrecy creates its own problems. When people sense something is happening behind closed doors, they fill in the blanks themselves—and usually with worst-case scenarios.

Transparent communication doesn't mean telling everyone everything on day one. It means having the right conversations at the right time, with the right people, in a way that builds trust and clarity rather than confusion or panic.

Start Early, Even If It's Uncomfortable

The biggest mistake owners make is waiting until everything is final before saying a word. But by then, it's often too late to build alignment—or to address resistance that could have been defused months earlier.

Staff members, especially long-tenured employees, don't need to know every deal term. But they do need to understand:
- That you are thinking about the future of the business
- That you are committed to a smooth and thoughtful transition
- That their jobs, clients, and culture are being considered

Even a simple statement like, "I'm beginning to think about what comes next for the business, and I want to make sure our transition—whenever it happens—is done carefully and with respect for the team," can build goodwill and reduce anxiety.

The same applies to your successor. Too many owners test the waters with vague, noncommittal language: "Maybe someday this could be yours." That creates ambiguity. It can also breed resentment if the successor assumes you're offering something you're not.

If someone is being seriously considered as a successor, they deserve a **clear conversation** about what you're thinking, what concerns you have, and what steps need to happen before anything becomes official. This isn't just about fairness—it's about alignment. A successor who feels included in the planning process is more likely to stay engaged, take ownership, and build trust with your team.

The Family Variable

If family is involved in your business—or expects to be—communication gets even more delicate. One of the most common succession landmines occurs when one child is selected to take over and others are left out, confused, or resentful.

Avoiding that conversation doesn't make it go away. It just ensures that feelings fester, relationships strain, and future legal battles become more likely. If your plan involves passing the business to one heir and not another, say so clearly. Explain why. Be generous, if you can, in finding ways to make things fair even if they can't be equal.

If you're not ready to have the conversation yourself, consider involving a neutral third party: an estate planning attorney, financial advisor, or business consultant who can frame the discussion without emotional baggage. In high-tension situations, even **family therapists or trained mediators** can be invaluable. These are not signs of dysfunction—they're tools for protecting relationships while working through high-stakes decisions.

Communicating with Clients and Vendors

Your customers, clients, and vendors don't need to know about your transition planning until the plan is real and the timeline is clear. But once that moment comes, **how** you communicate can make or break your successor's ability to retain business.

The worst thing you can do is quietly disappear.

Instead, craft a message that is calm, confident, and transitional in tone. Let clients know:

- You're proud of the business and committed to its continuity
- You've planned carefully and handpicked your successor
- You'll still be involved during the handoff
- Their experience and trust are valued and protected

Whenever possible, **introduce the successor personally,** either one-on-one or in small group settings. Give them credibility by transferring trust. And stay involved, even lightly, long enough to reassure clients that nothing is being abandoned or neglected.

Internal Communication Isn't a One-Time Event

The most effective transitions include an internal communication plan that unfolds gradually:

- Early heads-up to key employees
- Periodic updates as progress is made
- Clear explanations once the deal is finalized
- Ongoing reassurance during the transition phase

You don't need a corporate PR team to do this well. You just need empathy, honesty, and a willingness to engage.

Succession is not just a legal process—it's a relational one. You're not handing off a title; you're transferring **trust, responsibility, and legacy.** That doesn't happen through paperwork. It happens through conversation.

SECTION 5: YOU ARE NOT ALONE

If you've felt overwhelmed while reading this book, you're not failing—you're human.

Succession planning is hard. Not because the math is difficult or the legal work is impossible, but because the decisions involved strike at the core of your identity. You've spent years—maybe decades—building your business. Handing it off isn't just a financial transaction. It's personal.

The good news is: **you are not alone.**

Thousands of small business owners have stood exactly where you are now. They've faced the same fear of letting go, the same uncertainty about successors, the same doubts about whether their business is even worth passing on. And many of them have found a way through.

Some found successors within their team. Some trained children or nieces or nephews. Others transitioned to managers or long-time employees who never imagined they'd become owners until someone believed in them.

If you're stuck, support is out there. Business coaches, succession consultants, attorneys, financial planners—yes, they all have a role. But so do peers. Other business owners who have walked this path can offer powerful insight. Don't be afraid to ask questions. Don't be afraid to say, "I'm not sure what to do next."

You don't have to figure it out in isolation. You just have to stay committed to the process.

And if you're reading this thinking, *"I wish someone had written this book ten years ago,"*—that's exactly why it exists. Because someone else out there will one day need to hear your story, too.

SECTION 6: YOUR LEGACY IS A LIVING THING

When most people hear the word "legacy," they picture something frozen in time. A building with a plaque. A name etched in stone. But in small business, your legacy isn't static. **It's living.**

Every process you documented, every client you retained, every team member you mentored—that's legacy. And when you plan your exit thoughtfully, you're not walking away. You're passing something forward.

This book was never about retiring. It was about **transitioning with intention**—so the business you built can grow without you, thrive without you, and carry your values forward. That is your legacy. And you don't have to wait until your final day to see it take shape. You can start now.

You can witness your successor stepping into leadership. You can coach them through tough moments. You can see your business evolve, and know that it continues because of the decisions you made—not in spite of them.

You earned that.

The future of your business won't be a mirror image of the past—and that's okay. What matters is that it exists at all. That it endures. That it serves. That it lives.

And it will—because you chose not to leave that future to chance.

ACKNOWLEDGMENTS

This book would not have been possible without the support, insight, and encouragement of the people listed below.

Each of you, in your own way, helped me stay focused, solve problems, and keep going when things got hard. Thank you.

Terre Bridgham
Andrea Call
Bill Chertok
Patti Chertok
Alex Cuffe
Alexis English
Terri English
Rebecca English
Rick English
Tim English
Sharon Furman
Rick Frecska
Madeline Goodfellow
Alok Gupta
Kathy Hogan
Chelsea Jolton
Tasha Mcmanus
Daniel Ringquist
Steve Weeks

ABOUT THE AUTHOR

Victoria English is an entrepreneur, writer, and media creator with decades of experience across multiple industries. Drawing on her background in building and transitioning small businesses, she wrote **Internal Succession: Retirement Solutions for Small Business Owners** to help entrepreneurs protect their legacy and plan for the future. She lives in Los Angeles with her daughter, Madeline, and her partner, Rick.